COMMON GROUND

Coffee Shop Chronicles to Warm Your Heart and Soul

Jan Unfried

Cover designed by Jan Unfried

Follow Common Ground on Facebook @ commongroundchronicles

Printed in the United States of America

First Printing: September 2018
Independently Published by Jan Unfried

ISBN-978-1-7198-2690-7

There is nothing like writing your first book. Many people have been there for me through the ups and downs, the twists and turns, and the time and effort it has taken. I would have to include volumes to mention everyone who contributed to this project, and I know I would still miss some. I hope I will be able to thank many of you in person. For now, I would like to express my gratitude to a few who have greatly impacted my journey.

Jerry—my husband, for supporting my dream and giving me feedback along the way. Thank you for loving me through the past forty-two years and for being such a blessing in my life!

Patti King and Terie Storar—two of my dearest friends. Thank you for sharpening me as an author and as a person! I couldn't do life without you!

Pastor Darren Reed—Thank you for believing in me, encouraging this project, and giving me the opportunity to share my "God-idea" with you and our congregation.

My deepest gratitude to all who took the time to share your story with me. Without you this book wouldn't be possible.

My Lord and Savior, Jesus Christ, the Creator of all things—Thank you for being my eternal friend, my inspiration, and my joy.

GRAB YOUR BOOK,

FIND YOUR FAVORITE CHAIR,

BREW YOUR BEVERAGE OF CHOICE,

AND ENJOY SOME COMMON GROUND!

Jan Unfried

CONTENTS

INTRODUCTION

COFFEE! You may be a coffee lover or a coffee connoisseur. Maybe you don't like coffee at all. Perhaps you are somewhere in between. It doesn't really matter because *Common Ground* is not so much about coffee, but about the things that happen over a cup of coffee, or tea, or a coke. It's about relationships and God-ordained meetings. It's about God working in the common, ordinary places in our lives to create God-sized miracles!

Some of these stories came from my own experiences. Many were shared with me by dear friends, relatives, or new acquaintances. I am deeply grateful to all who opened their lives and their narratives to me. The bottom line is that each encounter provided unique insight into who God is.

I sincerely hope that you will get a glimpse into God's character as you read through these pages. Whether you read it in one sitting or over a series of days, I pray that you will see His faithfulness, His provision, and His pleasure in nurturing a relationship with you. My heart's desire is that you will gain a sense of His purpose, His love, and His direction for your life. I wait with anticipation to hear how the Holy Spirit has challenged you, prompted you, or strengthened you through the accounts that you have read. May you grasp all that God has in store for you as He intentionally pursues you and others in your circle of influence who need freedom, comfort, protection, or healing.

God cherishes each person! He longs to turn your sorrow into joy. He yearns to bring peace from your storm. He wants to use you where you are, in your specific location, job, school, or neighborhood. As you read about the work of God in other people's lives, stop and listen to what God is saying to you. Spend time studying the Scripture references and doing some self-reflecting.

To help you delve a little deeper, each chapter ends with a "Single-cup Summary," consisting of a set of bullet points listing key ideas from the chapter. Also included are correlated scripture references to look up and study on your own. These are listed as "Grounded in the Word." Finally, there is a page for your own reflections or journaling called "Points to Ponder and Percolate." Hopefully these will be helpful tools for digging into what God wants to say to you.

As we journey through *Common Ground* my prayer is that you might be inspired and challenged to deepen your walk with God, strengthen your relationship with those you already know, and have a renewed sense of reaching out to the lost in the world. As I prayed over each chapter, I asked God to permeate the stories with His message for you. My prayer continues to be that they would not be just a collection of nice stories, but they would be God's story. Welcome to these pages. Sit down with a cup of coffee and enjoy some **common ground**!

IN THE BEGINNING

In the beginning God created the heavens and the earth.
Genesis 1:1

My husband and I just returned from a road trip across the United States. We only took five and a half weeks to do it, so there was a lot we didn't' see. What we did see, however, left no doubt in my mind that there **is** a God who created the heavens and the earth! The diversity and beauty we experienced each day was incredible. Sometimes it was just the changing sky. We would start our morning enjoying spotty clouds, get caught mid-day in a torrential downpour, and spend the evening captivated by a vibrant sunset. At other times it was the varying of the terrain. Within a few hours we would revel in the majestic view of the snow-capped Rocky Mountains, then gaze in awe at fantastic rock formations in the Utah desert. The wildlife ranged from soaring eagles to herds of buffalo. The flora fluctuated from lush forests to cactus and Joshua trees.

In the minute details of creation, I believe that God, in His amazing creative and cerebral powers, made the coffee bean. On the third day, when He was separating the water from the dry ground and developing the intricacies of vegetation and seed-bearing plants and trees, He probably looked ahead and knew that once man discovered coffee, it would be a big hit! For centuries, however, it remained a hidden secret. So how did coffee come to be known?

Ethiopia is the original home of coffee, and the Ethiopians are very proud of this fact. The coffee plant first blossomed in the Ethiopian region of Kaffa, thus giving coffee its name.

> *According to Ethiopia's ancient history, an Abyssinian goatherd, Kaldi, who lived around AD 850, discovered coffee. He observed his goats prancing excitedly and bleating loudly after chewing the bright red berries that grew on some green bushes nearby. Kaldi tried a few berries himself, and soon felt a sense of elation. He filled his pockets with the berries and ran home to announce his discovery. At his wife's suggestion, he took the berries to the Monks in the monastery near Lake Tana, the source of the Blue Nile River.*
>
> *Kaldi presented the chief Monk with the berries and related his account of their miraculous effect. 'Devil's work' exclaimed the monk, and hurled the berries in the fire. Within minutes the monastery filled with the aroma of roasting beans, and the other monks gathered to investigate. The beans were raked from the fire and crushed to extinguish the embers. The chief Monk ordered the grains to be placed in the ewer and covered with hot water to preserve their goodness. That night the monks sat up drinking the rich fragrant brew, and vowed that they would drink it daily to keep them awake during their long, nocturnal devotions.[1]*

While this is a popular legend of how coffee was discovered, it is historic fact that people were chewing on the Ethiopian-grown berries long before they were brewed. They were used as a stimulant to help travelers stay alert during long journeys or to help

---

[1]"Ethiopian Coffee," *Selamta, The In-Flight Magazine of Ethiopian Airlines.* Volume 13, Number 2 April – June 1996 <http://www.selamta.net/Ethiopian%20Coffee.htm>

priests remain attentive during nightly prayer vigils. People began brewing coffee around AD 900, and the first "coffee houses" began in the mid-fifteenth century as a place to socialize and discuss political topics.

My brother-in-law, Dave, has had some first-hand experience with Ethiopians and their coffee ties. He travels internationally as Dean of T-Net Training Center, training local men and women to become leaders and pastors in their own countries. Because he is familiar with the people and their culture, he recently befriended their Minnesota bank teller, Seble, who is of Ethiopian origin. As their relationship developed, Dave asked if her family would want to come over for dinner. She accepted and agreed to bring a food from their country to share. A few days later, however, she asked if Dave and his wife, Jeannette, would come to her house instead. It was just easier for her to prepare the injera, a sourdough-risen flatbread, and the accompanying dishes at her own home.

Jeannette agreed to bring mashed potatoes, as requested by Seble and her three boys. They were introduced to Seble's mom, who spoke very little English, but whose countenance spoke love and joy. They also met the three bright and handsome boys. As the pre-dinner conversation ensued and more questions were being asked about their culture and faith, Seble and her family became excited. It was one of their holy weeks. They wanted Dave and Jeannette to watch some videos that explained some of their Coptic Orthodox Church traditions.

The meal was finally ready. The injera was placed before them, and they were taught how to eat Ethiopian fare. As you unroll a little piece of the injera, you use it to scoop up a bite of meat, beans, or vegetables. Without touching your fingers to your mouth, you pop the entire morsel in at once. Dave and Jeannette were fine with the fact that they provided the family with a bit of comic relief as they attempted the process.

After the meal they began the coffee ceremony, another Ethiopian tradition. This practice of hospitality begins with the actual roasting of the coffee beans on a flat pan over a charcoal brazier. The aroma of the beans roasting is part of the enticement of the experience as you wait for the coffee to be completed. Once roasted, the beans are ground and brewed in a special pot with a narrow spout. The strained coffee is poured in a stream from about a foot above the small cups from which the company will soon drink. It is typical for sugar to be offered, along with a 2nd and 3rd serving later in the evening. Grandma made sure Jeannette had plenty of sugar for her 2nd cup. Though not all the traditional apparatus was used, it was as authentic as they could make it in this modern American home.

A couple of months after this wonderful experience, Dave was given an invitation to return to Ethiopia for a few days to talk through their curriculum with their African team. Dave contacted Seble to see if she might want to send anything with him to her family in Ethiopia. The day before his flight, Seble, her mom, and the three boys brought a suitcase of goods to Dave and Jeannette's home.

After about an hour of touring their house, declaring the contents of the suitcase, and visiting, Seble asked if she could pray over Dave's trip before she and her family left. Each family member, beginning with the oldest boy, both of the twin boys, and then Seble, articulated God's blessing and favor over Dave and Jeannette. It was a God-breathed moment, a little taste of what it will be like in Heaven when we join together to worship Jesus with all cultures, nations, and races who have accepted Him as their Savior. We are one in Jesus (see Galatians 3:28)!

So in the beginning God created, amongst many glorious things, coffee. The stories begin here of how God and coffee bring people together and provide a place of **common ground**. In the end, the only thing that will matter is your relationship with the Creator of all things! Do you know Him? He desperately wants to know you and help you to become who He created you to be.

 ## Single-Cup Summary

- God created the heavens and the earth, including the coffee bean and all mankind.
- In Christ, all nations, cultures and races are one!
- The Creator wants to have a relationship with you.

 ## Grounded in the Word

- Genesis 1-2
- Galatians 3:26-28
- John 3:16
- Proverbs 3:5-6

Points to Ponder and Percolate

DO YOU LOVE ME MORE THAN THESE?

When they had finished eating, Jesus said to Simon Peter,
"Simon son of John, do you love me more than these?" John 21:15a

Every January our pastor challenges our congregation to an individual and corporate twenty-one days of prayer and fasting. We are encouraged to think beyond just a meal or meals, and to consider a specific food or food group, social media, television, or anything God would lead us to sacrifice. The point of fasting isn't to concentrate on how much we are suffering because of denying ourselves of something, but to focus on bringing glory to God through strengthening our relationship with him. Each year my husband and I pray and discuss what we feel God is asking us to give up for the three week period. Sometimes we fast the same thing, and other times we feel led in different directions.

In 2018, we had decided to give up sweets. Coming off of the recent holidays, we knew we would definitely hit a sugar low! The sacrifice was primarily about denying the habit of going for a treat, and we were sure the first few days would be especially tough. The fast was to begin on a Sunday, and we would end with a good old-fashioned church soup and bread potluck three Sundays later to celebrate the end of the fast. I could already taste the sweet desserts that would be part of the festivities.

A few weeks earlier I had a providential appointment with my hair dresser, who is an amazing woman of God, a confidante, and special friend who attends the same church as I do. She and I committed to read Mark Batterson's *Draw the Circle, The 40 Day Prayer Challenge.* We agreed to circle our pastor and our church body in prayer for twenty-one days as we read through the book.

On the Monday after the fast began, as I was reading the Bible and praying with a cup of coffee in hand, I heard God say to my spirit that he wanted me to fast coffee. I passed it off as a case of mistaken revelation. Then I heard him say, almost audibly, "Do you love me more than coffee?" I chuckled to myself, and answered, "Of course I do! How ridiculous!" He answered me, "Then, give up coffee for me."

I would like to tell you that I immediately obeyed this still small voice, but I actually went one more day enjoying my morning coffee. I became so heavily convicted, that I conceded to relinquishing my coffee habit for the remaining nineteen days. It really wasn't about the caffeine, although I did get a terrible headache for a couple of days. It was more about the comfort and taste that centered around that cup of Joe. Tea just didn't do it for me. I missed the morning cup with my devotions—I was convinced it helped me concentrate more on God. I missed the fellowship I felt with my husband or other coffee drinkers as we would sip and share. I missed the occasional afternoon treat that helped fuel the rest of the day. Every time I smelled coffee or was around coffee or saw someone drinking coffee on TV, I pined for it.

The only one I shared with about my coffee fast was my husband. He laughed—I don't know if he thought it was silly or that I wouldn't be able to do it. However, God was teaching me that to love and seek Him was all that mattered. He would take care of the rest. When we put him first, we receive so much more than we can even envision (see Matthew 6:33). He continually provides comfort and warmth. He fosters fellowship and relationship with us, and He gives us others to walk through life's journey with us. He gives us the perfect fuel of joy, peace, strength, or whatever we need for our trek through life. The bottom line is, He fills our cup to overflowing (see Psalm 23:5)!

Fast forward to Day 9 of *Draw the Circle*. Batterson was sharing about his church's coffee house that had been dedicated to the Lord. He was writing about a gentleman whose dream was born and fostered in that coffee house, and about how this gentleman is now touching millions of lives. It had started with a church member's prayer during the dedication of the building that God would make their coffee house a "dream factory" for God ideas.

As I read, I began to inexplicably cry. Was God calling me to create some type of a coffee house at our church? Maybe that was the reason God had called me to fast coffee. I am a teacher by career. I have no real business sense or any idea how to create a business plan. But I wrote it down, circled the dream, and prayed for continued clarification of this God-idea. If this was where God was leading, it would definitely have to come from Him. It would take a God-sized miracle. I rested the idea in God's hands.

A couple of days later, I was struck with the thought that instead of a physical space housing a coffee shop, I was to write a book with chapters that would tell how God met with people over a cup of coffee. The idea grew as I began to jot down some of my own experiences and list people I could interview who used a coffee house or lunch spot to connect with others. I even found a 2002 article that I had written that could be included as a chapter. I realized that my dream of writing a book had been percolating for many years, and God was pushing the brew button.

I began to toss around some possible titles. Some early title contenders were a little cheesy, like *Java with Jesus.* During the Sunday morning of breaking the fast, Pastor Darren, the senior pastor at Olive Knolls Nazarene Church, shared his heart for our church to be FOR our city and community, just as God is FOR us. He admonished us to reach out to the lost, encourage the businesses and neighbors around us expecting nothing in return, and keep our focus on the reason why we are doing it—to share the love of JESUS. Here were his 3 main points as to how we could begin:

1) Create **Common Ground**
2) Create Conversations
3) Create Connections

The first point from the notes practically jumped out at me from the screen! I elbowed my husband, who gave me a strange look. I'm sure he wondered if he had fallen asleep and started snoring. I circled the words "Common Ground." I whisper-shouted to him (you know what I mean if you've ever been excited about something during a church service), "This should be the title of my book!" It was one more confirmation that as I wrote about people connecting over coffee grounds, the stories they told would be used of God to inspire and motivate those reading them.

After the first service, I went up to the pastor. I usually don't try to talk to the pastor between services because I know that he needs to get ready for the next group coming in. I just was too excited! I gave him the short version of my journey thus far, and we agreed to meet. There was something in his eyes that said there was more to this than I could have imagined.

A couple of weeks went by before we both had time in our schedule. In the meantime, we had the opportunity to hear from Amanda one Sunday in February. Amanda came up through our youth group, and is now following her dream to help a community in Uganda. I didn't know she was back in town, but God had brought her to my mind earlier in the week. I had prayed for her and her ministry. As she shared in the morning service at our church, she talked about having fasted coffee. She articulated a dream God had given her to start a coffee house in the town where she lived in order to create a self-sustainable funding source for some of their other ministries.

Of course, my spiritual senses heightened as she spoke. God's providence had brought Amanda to my thoughts earlier in the week, and now he was putting her into my path! Here was another person who had been given a God-vision via coffee. Don't get me wrong. I'm not trying to over-spiritualize coffee itself. It's just that when God begins a work in you, He consistently shows you how His power and purpose far out-reaches anything we can think or imagine. (You can read more about Amanda's story in Ch. 3.)

I finally had the opportunity to sit down with the pastor and share my thoughts. He saw the coffee house for our community as a viable idea, one that would fit in with other visions he had for the church's future. He said that more than one person had presented the seed thought of a coffee house to him, and he didn't see it as just a coincidence that people from different walks of life were feeling similar stirrings from God. We had a great conversation about the stories for this book, and he gave me some ideas as to how to proceed.

If you are reading these pages, then you know that God continued to pave the way. I have no doubt in my mind that God called me to be involved in the privilege of hearing some amazing stories from some incredible people. He calls each one of us in a unique way. I encourage you to ask what it is God is calling you to do for Him. If you seek Him, He will reveal Himself to you. He can use a variety of methods and means to plant His dreams in your heart. He wants you to be excited about what excites him. When we yield ourselves to His will, when we become uber-aware of ways He is working, when we see that our small sacrifices for Him can multiply into an abundance in our lives, we can't help but be excited.

Jesus asked Peter, "Do you love me more than these?" How is Jesus filling in "these" for your life? Is it coffee, technology, work, family? When you yield that which is near and dear to your heart, God will begin to show you His heart. Get ready for Him to launch you on a journey full of joy and miracles!

Single-Cup Summary

- Fasting and praying focuses us on bringing glory to God in our circumstances and strengthening our relationship with Him.
- When we put God first, we receive so much more than we can imagine.
- When we allow God to guide us, His goodness and love overflows in our lives.
- We are each called by God to serve Him in unique and purposeful ways.
- When we yield that which is near and dear to our heart, God will begin to show us His heart.

 Grounded in the Word

- John 21:15-19
- Matthew 6:33
- Psalm 23:5-6
- Ephesians 3:20-21

Points to Ponder and Percolate

_____

_____

_____

_____

_____

_____

_____

_____

_____

_____

_____

_____

_____

_____

_____

_____

_____

_____

_____

_____

_____

_____

_____

HE OWNS THE CATTLE ON A THOUSAND HILLS

For every animal of the forest is mine, and the cattle on a thousand hills. Psalm 50:10

This passage from Psalm 50 has often been used as an illustration of God's promise of provision. In the context of the rest of the passage, however, we find a profound call to sacrifice thank offerings and worship Him genuinely without expecting anything in return. In his second letter to the Corinthians, Paul encourages us to be cheerful givers. He admonishes that whoever "sows generously will also reap generously" (see 2 Corinthians 9:6). When we give in this way, God is able to make sure that grace and good works will abound, and our needs will be met (see 2 Corinthians 9:8). Our rewards for serving and giving reach far beyond material blessings. He wants to shower us with grace and enrich our harvest of righteousness.

Amanda Johnson is a great testament to serving and giving. I briefly introduced you to Amanda in chapter two. She was part of my "coffee" journey, and I knew she had a great story to tell. As we sat around a cup of coffee, Amanda began to unfold her testimony. She admitted that she was a rebellious teenager. Many of us had joined her mom in prayer for her during some of those tough years. Our oldest son did a summer internship at our church as a junior high pastor during the summer before Amanda's freshman year in high school. The back-and-forth banter between the two of them was fun and light, but the underlying message Amanda received from him and others was that neither we nor God were going to let go of her! She was being hedged in by the love and prayers of many. Amanda was going to be the recipient of grace and produce a bountiful harvest of righteousness.

Amanda had gone on several mission trips with the youth group during high school. When the opportunity to go to South Africa came along, Amanda adamantly decided she was not going to go. Later in college, another opportunity came along to go to Rwanda, but she didn't go then either. God was nudging her to try Africa, but she wasn't "ready." During the spring break before graduating from college with a psychology degree, Amanda decided to take some friends up on an offer to visit them at Liberty University, in Lynchburg, Virginia. She absolutely loved the campus community and applied for graduate school there during her visit.

She soon got word that she had been accepted into grad school at Liberty for the fall of 2013. She moved to Virginia, began attending classes, and through a mutual friend, met a guy named Collin. One day Collin was talking about going to Uganda in May of 2014, and he invited Amanda to go along. Again her answer was no. When May rolled around, Amanda felt like God was telling her that she had missed an opportunity. She promised God that if Collin went again, she would go with him. Little did she know what God had in store.

A few months later, Amanda found herself at the Central California Nazarene Family Camp. There is something holy and sacred about this camp. It's not the place, but the memories and the altars that have been built there in response to God's calling. Many of our church families take their kids or grandkids every summer as a sacrifice of thanksgiving to God. There are many other vacation destinations that are much more glamorous. There are a lot of other places that would make taking a week off of work seem worth the time and effort. But here at Camp Sugar Pine in the Sierra Nevada Mountains, kids have a week to be part of a bigger picture, maybe even to get a little glimpse into heaven. They have so much fun hanging out with their friends, being given a little bit of extra freedom in a safe environment. They connect with past acquaintances and meet new friends. They watch as those from little children to senior adults commit their lives to God in refreshing ways.

It was in this setting that Amanda heard a call from God. The pastor at the evening service under the stars was preaching about Abraham and Isaac. He posed the question, "What is the Isaac in your life that you need to sacrifice? What do you need to give up in order to do what God has called you to do?" As she pondered these questions, she realized she was holding tightly to comfort and security. In Amanda's words, "I knew for me, at this moment, [my sacrifice] meant dropping out of school, quitting my job, and going to Uganda."

She continued to vacillate about her decision for the next few weeks. The next semester was approaching and she was still enrolled in her classes. A week before the semester started, she dropped all her classes. She still questioned herself: "What did I just do?" From there, things began to fall into place. Amanda began meeting weekly with Collin, who was excited to have a partner in his planning. They originally planned to go to Africa for a 9-month mission trip, visiting a different country each month. God spoke to them both at separate times, telling them to start a non-profit organization. They spent some time researching the process, and God provided the people they needed to help them with all of the details. They actually applied for their non-profit status in March of 2015. They heard back in regards to their status in April. That kind of turn-around for the application for non-profit status in unheard of! In most cases it can take up to two years. With God giving them all of the green lights, they created their name, Unified in Mission, and built their website.

Uganda was to be their first stop along the way. As soon as they landed in Uganda, Amanda knew this is where she wanted to be. The town where they eventually settled is called Rukungiri. The people she met were some of the most hospitable people she had ever known. They were hosted by the North Kigezi Diocese, the church of Uganda under Britain's colonization. This church body had many of the same goals for community development, youth empowerment and job creation as Collin and Amanda. Obedience was the first step. The step became a leap of faith as God continued to work. For Amanda it was like Peter stepping out of the boat or the children of Israel setting foot in the Red Sea **before** it parted.

It soon became evident that they were to stay in Rukungiri. Part of their ministry is to host teams from the United States to experience Uganda and share in what God is doing through *Unified In Mission*. Teams have helped build schools, water tanks, and the current training center. God also brought local partners into their lives. They are able to work with a variety of organizations in the town and country to further their work.

So often non-profit organizations unintentionally "compete" with each other. *Unified in Mission* lives up to its name.

They unify with others from abroad and locally to become stronger in their goals. One of the accomplishments so far has been the building of a school which houses more than two hundred students. Education is important to the Ugandans, and Amanda is passionate about making this a safe place where students can be challenged academically and creatively. Of course, the building is just the first step. They need continued help in maintaining supplies and providing scholarships.

The training center is another special project, which also needs ongoing funds to sustain its purpose. One of Amanda's prayers was that the training center could be self-supporting. That's when God put the idea of a coffee house on Amanda's heart. The coffee house would be a way to create jobs. Local people could be trained as baristas or managers. They could contract with local dairy farmers for their milk products, creating a sustainable and consistent business for them. Uganda's main export is coffee. They would be able to contract with the local coffee farmers, roasters, and processors, to utilize their products in the store.

Another reason she is so passionate about a coffee house is because she is passionate about her relationship with Christ. She said that even though the Ugandan's know about God and the Bible through the church, they lack the relationship side of their walk with God. When it comes to knowing Jesus, they don't necessarily receive the encouragement to develop their friendship with Him. She sees this coffee shop as a hub for creating **common ground** and building relationships with people. With a location for the community to gather, she could host men's and women's Bible studies, have a place for people to learn to apply God's Word and ask important questions, and accommodate worship teams to play live music.

As Amanda prayed about the coffee shop, Kiki entered her life. Kiki had been to Uganda a couple of times, but it seemed to always be when Amanda was back at home. When their paths finally crossed, they met over coffee in California to share their mutual vision. Kiki was God's perfect partner for this venture. She had the educational background and knowledge to put together a business plan, a financial plan, the menu, and supplies. Their big picture dream is to someday have their own coffee plantation and their own dairy cows. These undertakings would be additional ways to provide jobs and training for the local people, while bringing in the income to help fund other projects.

Amanda and Collin never left Rukungiri, Uganda. God placed them there for a reason. Amanda gave up everything—her education, her job, her career—to follow God's will for her life. When I asked her how she made her living—food, lodging, travel back and forth to the states—she smiled and just said, "It's all God." She and Collin use just what is needed from their fund raising efforts to sustain a basic life style, but they don't earn a paycheck from the donations. It is inexpensive compared to the states to live there, so the vast majority of funding goes into the education and training centers. To fly back and forth to the states, God placed a miracle in their lives they had not specifically asked for. A man from Bakersfield who is very mission-minded, but who cannot go to the mission fields himself, decided to do his own fundraising for money to purchase plane tickets for missionaries. He met with Amanda and agreed to pay for her and Collin's flights to and from the United States when needed.

Amanda has given to God the ultimate sacrifice—her time and herself. He is rewarding her with provisions she didn't even know to ask for. He does own the cattle on a thousand hills. He can work though the hearts of those who have been blessed financially to help His work continue. Their goal is to eventually be self-sustainable and not have to fund raise. God can do it! In the meantime, some of us have the privilege of partnering with them*. As they work toward their dreams, God can provide the plantation, the employees, the funds, and even the milk cows (on a thousand hills).

Like Abraham, we all have Isaacs in our lives--people or things that are precious and dear to our hearts. God is asking us to give Him those things that are seemingly impossible to release. Then He can bless us beyond our wildest imaginations! There is nothing too big for God. He asks for our all, which seems too risky, too scary. In the long run, whether we are sent to Uganda or we work in our own back yard, our sacrifice of thanksgiving will produce an amazing harvest of righteousness.

*If you are interested in finding out more about *Unified in Mission*, donating to their organization, or being part of a mission team, go to https://unifiedinmission.org/

 Single-Cup Summary

- God desires genuine offering and worship from us.

- When we give generously, God not only meets our needs, but He showers us with grace and a harvest of righteousness.
- God calls us to let go of the things we hold onto so tightly in order for us to receive His blessings.
- Our obedience often involves a leap of faith.

 Grounded in the Word

- Psalm 50:7–15
- 2 Corinthians 9:6–11
- Genesis 22:1–18
- Matthew 14:22–32

 *Points to Ponder and Percolate*

CHAPLAIN OF ST. ARBUCKS

He determines the number of the stars and calls them each by name. Psalm 147:4

A recent study indicates that infants are sensitive to their own name as early as four months. As shown by their brain activity, they differentiate between their name and those with similar sounds and phonemes. Our names are important! We respond immediately when someone calls our name. If someone remembers our name it provides validation and affirms our worth. When someone uses our name, we feel like they know us.

As Creator of the Universe, God knows the importance of calling us by name. He calls each star by name. That is incredibly beyond our capability as humans to comprehend. As our Great Shepherd, God knows and calls all of his sheep by name (see John 10:3). He goes beyond that and even knows the number of hairs on our head (see Matthew 10:30). He knows us intimately and calls us to Himself. He who calls us is faithful (see 1 Thessalonians 5:24). He knows exactly what we need and He calls us:

- Out of darkness into his wonderful light (see 1 Peter 2:9)
- To his eternal glory (see 1 Peter 5:10)
- To peace (see Colossians 3:15)

- To hope (see Ephesians 4:4)
- To grace (see Galatians 1:15)
- To freedom (see Galatians 5:13)
- To be holy (see I Corinthians 1:2)
- To belong (see Romans 1:6)
- To His purpose (see Romans 8:28)
- To be healed (see Mark 10:49-52)

Take a minute and put your name in front of each of these statements. It's almost impossible not to be completely overwhelmed with His goodness!

My friend Larry heard and answered when God called his name. He answered God's call to seek forgiveness for his sins. He answered God's call to the Lordship of Christ in his life. He answered God's call to ministry. And 10 years ago, my retired seventy-six-year-young friend, Larry, answered another call from God. In October of 2007 God called him by name and told him to go to his local Starbucks. Larry obeyed. When he wondered what he was supposed to do, God just told him, "Don't worry about it, just show up." He began making this his destination each morning from 5:20 – 7:15 AM.

As he sat with his coffee and the newspaper, he began to notice another gentleman who came each morning at about the same time. A few weeks passed before God prompted Larry to introduce himself. As Larry puts it, "Ten years ago, our lives changed." Dwayne was another believer, and they struck up a friendship and cultivated a mission field together. As people come in, they greet them with a smile. They get to know them by name. They build relationships, pray with people, and help draw some of God's sheep into His freedom, grace, peace, and hope. Their group of two has expanded to a core of about six who meet together to pray and watch God work.

Larry has had the privilege of marrying some of the couples he has met in Starbucks. He has ministered to those who are hurting. He and the others have been an encouragement and lifeline to those who have been in places of despair. A local pastor who came in for his morning coffee opened up to Larry and Dwayne. Even pastors need to be able to share their burdens with others at times. He recognized that they could listen to him objectively and lovingly. They could help him bear the load he was carrying. A few days later this pastor told Larry that he had a new name for him. He nicknamed him the chaplain of St. Arbucks. We chuckled over Larry's new title, but marveled at the implications it had.

Larry has developed a relationship with a local nut farmer, named Gary, who comes in every morning about 6:00. They talk about how the business is going and share prayer requests. Their core group of 6 ministers to people from all walks of life. There are teachers, nurses, business women and men, divorcees, and single moms. Sometimes Larry just senses that there is more to someone's story. When the person is agreeable to it, one of the group will sit down or take that person outside to hold hands and pray. Each of the six in the core group has unique strengths, and each one builds **common ground** with certain individuals because of his or her own background and experiences.

Larry and his group of prayer warriors have witnessed a love story or two. Two individuals that they talked to frequently, and who came in regularly, eventually met each other. The two of them were star-struck at Starbucks. They fell in love and became engaged. They asked Larry to perform their wedding ceremony. He would have loved to do it, but he was in Hawaii during their wedding date. Though that wedding didn't work out for him, he did perform another wedding. One day a lady who came in daily on the way to her job at the Little Red School House asked Larry if he would marry her and her fiancé. He did, and they are happily married to this day. It blesses him so much when he runs into them and can catch up on their lives.

About two years ago, a lady named Carol was introduced to the group. She was devastated by her husband suddenly leaving her and her 3 kids. She was beside herself. Alcoholism was involved, but she had not seen this coming. Their group encouraged her to start attending church. She did, and was baptized. They agreed in prayer for her husband's healing and reconciliation for the marriage. He graduated from Teen Challenge in March of 2018. Their marriage and family has been healed, and she and her boys were able to attend his graduation ceremony. God called Carol by name through this group into freedom and hope! Now that's a love story!!!

Another part of the Starbuck's ministry is with the baristas. One of the young ladies who works there is twenty-five-year-old Jenny. She sits down with Larry almost every morning during her "lunch break." It is a story of the complexities of life. Jenny was born into a family with five siblings. Each sibling has a different father. There is no connection with any of the immediate family members. Her grandmother took her on as a very young child and has raised her. Grandma encouraged her to continue with school and work hard. They attend church together and make it through the good times and bad times with each other and the Lord. Now the tables have turned and Jenny has become her caregiver. Larry has been able to pray with Jenny and encourage her in her walk with the Lord.

Emily is an interesting inter-generational relationship that has developed. She and Larry go to the same church, and they had met briefly because Larry knew her dad from a previous job. Emily is a Kindergarten teacher who stopped in at Starbucks on her way to work. She reached out to Larry and began to join the morning coffee klatch. They both cherish the time they can spend together.

A "wow moment" that Larry shared was with Geraldo, a worker of a gardening service who often shows up to get his early morning coffee. Geraldo is a man of God. He comes in to fuel up, shoot the breeze, and sometimes ask for prayer. He often brings in some of his co-workers, but one day he brought in his younger brother, Nicholas. Nicholas is chained by addiction to meth. Larry began to pray for Nicholas. Geraldo began having Nicholas come over and give Larry a hug. Larry used the opportunity to speak love and support into his life. He would tell him, "Jesus loves you." Nicholas and Larry would occasionally read a devotional together, and Larry actually got Nicholas his own Bible. One morning Geraldo came in alone. Nicholas had gone back to his drugs. He was out on the streets yet again. Larry continues to intercede for this boy and his brother. God is not done with Nicholas! In the meantime, He continues to do a work in Larry and Geraldo, building their faith and allowing them to stand in the gap for this young man as long as it takes. God is a God of hope!

Larry is in awe of what God is doing. He says his prayer every morning is for God to show up. It is not about him. He just wants to be used by God. He says it's walking with people in life as they walk through life's journeys. It's been the venue where everyone feels safe because it's not church. It's about relationships and calling others by name. Larry says calling someone by name changes the level of their relationship.

Are you listening for God's call on your life? What is He calling you to do? Who is He calling you to love? He longs to cultivate a relationship with you, and He has a name of someone who may not hear about Jesus unless you heed His call.

 ## Single-Cup Summary

- God knows each of us intimately and calls us by name.
- God knows what we need, and He calls us to Himself in order to restore and refresh us.
- God is a God of hope!
- God calls us to love others He has placed in our lives.

 ## Grounded in the Word

- Psalm 147:4
- John 10:3
- Matthew 10:30
- 1 Thessalonians 5:24
- 1 Peter 2:9
- 1 Peter 5:10
- Colossians 3:15
- Ephesians 4:4
- Galatians 1:15
- Galatians 5:13
- 1 Corinthians 1:2
- Romans 1:6
- Romans 8:28
- Mark 10:49-52
- Luke 10:27

Points to Ponder and Percolate

THE REST OF THE STORY

Because of the Lord's great love we are not consumed, for his compassions never fail. They are new every morning; great is your faithfulness. Lamentations 3:22-23

In the 1970's Paul Harvey premiered his own series, *The Rest of the Story*, on the ABC Radio Network. He would highlight little-known or forgotten facts on a variety of subjects, holding back his punch line or key element of the story until the end. He would conclude the segment with his famous tag line, "And now you know the rest of the story."

In chapter four you were introduced to the chaplain of St. Arbucks, Larry. One of the relationships that came from his mornings of waiting on God and connecting with others was a somewhat unlikely one. One morning at church a twenty-four-year-old young lady came up to Larry and introduced herself. Apparently she was finishing her elementary teaching credential, was new in town, and didn't know a lot of people. The **common ground** the two of them had was that Larry had worked with her dad in prior years. Her name was Emily, and here is "the rest of the story."

One morning after the initial introduction at church, Emily went by Starbucks to get a cup of coffee and saw Larry leaving. She was surprised to see him, and they stopped to chat. Larry told her that he came every morning and stayed for a couple of hours. Eventually Emily started occasionally joining the Starbucks group, which spanned in age from twenty-something to eighty. When she moved to a location closer to this Starbucks and her job, she began to be one of the regulars.

Larry and his wife were like grandpa and grandma to Emily. She would go and crash on their couch, take a nap, or watch television. It was a safe haven and a place to rest. Larry also helped her with all kinds of home projects like putting together furniture, hanging shelves, and hauling things in his truck for her. She mentioned how she treasures the times she has been able to spend with Larry and his wife, and how the time at Starbucks in the mornings has become something she looks forward to daily.

What strikes me as interesting about this story is God's great love, compassion, and faithfulness. He orchestrated Emily's move to Bakersfield from San Diego. He knew years ago that Emily would be living in the same town as her dad's former co-worker. God understood the holes that would need to be filled in Emily's life through relationships. He worked through one of the Starbuck's family to get Emily her first teaching job. She now enjoys the benefits of inter-generational wisdom and insight at the start of each day. Emily said that she just likes starting her day this way. It is new and refreshing every morning.

There's the friendly teasing about Larry's weakening hearing or Louie's driving through the stop sign outside their window's view. There is Cheryl, everyone's "mom," who brings an afternoon meal for the barista who has had a long shift. There's Dwayne who shows genuine interest in Emily's students and fills her in on the world's news. There's Pam and Carol and countless others who God uses to brighten Emily's day.

The thing is, Emily probably doesn't realize what she means to the others in return. She listens and learns about their families. She and the others mourn and pray with Geraldo when his brother falls off the wagon. She rejoices with them when God has answered prayer, restored a relationship, or filled a need. They all keep track of each other and know when one of their own is sick, on vacation, or having a day of golf. Each morning over their coffees or teas, God is renewing His faithfulness to this little remnant of His fold.

Emily knew I had already interviewed Larry. As Emily and I talked she would ask if Larry had already told me about a particular person or event. Most of the time it was a familiar account, but I wanted to hear it from another perspective. I wanted to hear "the rest of the story."

Each person in this sunrise Starbuck's group could spread dawn on additional viewpoints regarding the rich relationships and tidbits of material from their morning assemblies. Just as God creates distinctive sunrises every day, He weaves His story and His love for us through creative and matchless avenues. For Emily, her story doesn't end with the meetings at Starbucks.

Emily ministers to her Kindergarteners each day. She pours her love and life and gifts into them, spreading God's joy through her smiles and gentle guidance. She also works with the teen group at her church. Her summers are much more than two and a half months off of work. She works as a camp counselor. She travels with the teens as a sponsor on their mission trips. She works with a small group throughout the year and imparts wisdom and grace into teen girls' lives.

Who has God woven into your life? You cannot minimize the importance of your relationships. There may be someone you need to call or write a note of thanks to who has influenced your life in some way. Perhaps someone is feeling consumed by loneliness, fear, or frustration, and God wants you to be the conduit of His love and compassion. It doesn't matter if they are older, younger, or similar in age. Through you, God can show His faithfulness to someone else. His love and compassions never fail!

Reflect today on God's unfailing and unchanging character. One translation of the word "meditate is "to muse," a word related to "music." Some of our best thoughtful ponderings and worship of God are through songs that bring glory and honor to Him. Meditate on the words to an old hymn, "Great is Thy Faithfulness:"

Great is Thy faithfulness,
Oh, God, my Father.
There is no shadow of turning with Thee.
Thou changest not,
Thy compassions, they fail not.
As Thou hast been, Thou forever wilt be.

Great is Thy faithfulness.
Great is Thy faithfulness.
Morning by morning new mercies I see.
All I have needed Thy hand hath provided—
Great is Thy faithfulness,
Lord, unto me!

Single-Cup Summary

- God is loving, compassionate, and faithful.
- God weaves His story and His love for us through many different avenues.
- God uses us to show His love and faithfulness to others in our lives.
- It is important to meditate on God's goodness and faithfulness daily.

 Grounded in the Word

- Lamentations 3:22-23
- Matthew 5:13-16
- Psalm 77:11-15

Points to Ponder and Percolate

_____

_____

_____

_____

_____

_____

_____

_____

_____

_____

_____

_____

_____

_____

_____

_____

_____

_____

_____

_____

_____

_____

_____

_____

_____

_____

_____

PARTY CRASHER

In the same way, I tell you, there is rejoicing in the presence of the angels of God over one sinner who repents. Luke 15:10

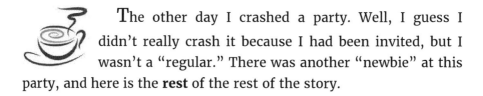The other day I crashed a party. Well, I guess I didn't really crash it because I had been invited, but I wasn't a "regular." There was another "newbie" at this party, and here is the **rest** of the rest of the story.

At the end of my talk with Emily about the group she meets with at Starbucks each morning, she told me I should come join them some time. The following Tuesday morning my regular Bible study group was taking the week off for spring break. I unsuccessfully tried to gather a few to meet for coffee. They were out of town or had to be at work early, so I texted Emily and let her know I was thinking about showing up. She encouraged me to come to experience it for myself.

When I arrived there were five people already sharing **common ground**. Larry and Dwayne sat in their normal spots, with Emily in between. On the other side of the table was Carol and Henry. I was quickly introduced and felt immediately welcomed. Since I was a newcomer, Larry offered to buy my coffee. With my Pike Place roast poured and doctored with just the right amount of cream, I sat down and joined in the conversation.

We visited for about an hour, and I could see how this group would easily become as addictive a morning routine as the caffeine they consume. A few people stopped by the table after picking up their drink to say, "Hi," and exchange a few words about the past week or their upcoming day. Like reported earlier, Larry greeted people with a smile, calling them by name. Carol told me, with a grin, about Larry's book. She made him show me where he had people's names written down with a brief description of them so he wouldn't forget—a brilliant idea, by the way.

After I left, Emily texted me and thanked me for coming. She reminded me of Carol's story. Her husband was the one who had been at Teen Challenge this past year. He had just finished the program, and Carol was bringing him to meet her morning support and prayer group. Suddenly, some of the conversations of the morning began to come together for me. Carol and Henry had just come back from a road trip to Oregon and Stockton to see their boys. Of course, Henry would want to share his journey with his sons and hopefully begin the healing and restoration of any broken relationships. It made sense that he was the other "newbie" that had joined us.

My husband sang for over twenty-five years in a gospel quartet called RSV. One of their early recordings included Gaither Vocal Band's "That's When the Angels Rejoice." The song talks about some of man's greatest accomplishments: the Golden Gate Bridge, the Wright brother's first flight, Thomas Edison's discovery of the lightbulb, the invention of the Model T, man stepping on the moon. For all those great feats, the angels do not have a party. The chorus goes on to say:

There's only one thing that we're sure about

That can make those angels jump and shout
It's when a sinner heeds the Savior's voice
That's when the angels rejoice

I didn't see any angels with us at our early morning meeting, but I bet they were crashing our party as well. They have probably been dancing and jumping and shouting for days in celebration of this one precious one who turned from his chains of addiction to the One who was calling him.

Our church has a grand tradition. When we have a baptismal service, we cheer and shout as the baptism candidates come up from being immersed in the water. It is better than Super Bowl Sunday or the World Series! We rejoice with those who are publicly declaring their regeneration in Christ. Many of their testimonies, from the young children to the adults, bring tears to my eyes.

At a recent baptism service, I chuckled as a couple of the elementary aged boys talked about trusting God through all the problems they have faced in their lives. How sweet that they are trusting God early and will be saved from great heartache of living in disobedience and separation from God. One nine-year-old had an especially mature testimony that ended with his very youthful comment, "And I just want to say, God rocks!" Woohoo!

The adults and teens often have been through a bit more of the world's trials. It truly is a celebration to hear how God has worked in their lives to bring them to a place of humility before Him and complete reliance on Him for their salvation.

I'm sure the angels are leading the party and cheering every time one of us stubborn sheep repents and makes a decision to follow

Jesus. I don't know about you, but that's the type of party I want to crash! Let's continue to be diligent in our prayer and outreach to the lost. God is concerned for each one who has not found their way to Him. He commissioned us, His followers, to share the Good News to those around us. We can start by building relationships and inviting others into our lives through **common ground**. Let's keep in perspective what is really important in life, and vow to be party crashers. I'm pretty sure the angels won't mind if we join in!

 ## Single-Cup Summary

- The angels rejoice over even one sinner who repents!
- We should be in the habit of rejoicing over victories in Christ, whether our own, or those of someone else.
- God is concerned for each one who has not found their way to Him.
- We are commissioned to share the Good News to those around us.

 ## Grounded in the Word

- Luke 15:10
- Romans 12:15
- Luke 15:1-9
- 2 Corinthians 5:20-21

Points to Ponder and Percolate

A SWEET AROMA

For we are to God the aroma of Christ among those who are being saved and those who are perishing. 2 Corinthians 2:15

There is nothing that can conjure up an appetite quite like the smell of baking bread. If you have ever walked past a bakery when bread was being pulled from the ovens, you were most likely overwhelmed with the desire to purchase some morsels on the spot. Bread has been a staple food in our diets for centuries. Leavened or unleavened, bread is historically the oldest recorded artificial food. We know God saw the value in bread because it is mentioned multiple times in the Bible, and bread is used symbolically throughout Jewish and Christian traditions.

In Exodus 23 we find the initiation of the Feast of Unleavened Bread as a remembrance of the night the Israelites fled from Egypt. The lack of yeast was to signify the haste with which God's people had to flee from Pharaoh's grasp. Later in Exodus, when giving instructions for items to be placed in the Holy Place in the Tabernacle, God commanded that the bread of the Presence be placed before Him at all times. The children of Israel received manna throughout their desert wanderings to learn total dependence on the Lord. The lesson was clear that "...man does not live by bread alone, but on every word that comes from the mouth of the Lord" (Deuteronomy 8:3b).

In the New Testament we see additional uses and applications of bread. In the Gospels Jesus used Deuteronomy 8:3 in response to the devil's temptation for him to turn stones into bread. Jesus taught us to pray, "Give us today our daily bread" (Matthew 6:11). He recognized the need of the crowds who came to listen to Him teach, and He multiplied the bread and fish of a young boy to feed thousands. He also recognized that the needs of the people went so much deeper than the physical. They were hungering for something that would be of eternal worth and that only He could give. In that moment Jesus declared, "I am the bread of life. He who comes to me will never go hungry, and he who believes in me will never be thirsty" (John 6:35).

In Christian tradition we worship the Lord through communion as he modeled for us on the night He was betrayed. At the Last Supper with His disciples, Jesus took bread, gave thanks for it, broke it, and said, "This is my body which was broken for you; do this in remembrance of me" (1 Corinthians 11:24b). Similarly He took the cup and told us to take it in remembrance of His shed blood for us. Something as common and familiar to us as bread takes on incredible meaning through the practicality and imagery it imbues.

Bread absolutely holds significance in our lives. Even those with gluten intolerance will search for the best tasting gluten-free breads. Add a little sugar and cinnamon, and you now have ever popular pastries. Offices make Friday doughnut runs. Many local grocery stores include a fresh bakery as part of their marketing, well stocked with homemade cookies, cakes, and pies. The bakery challenges on television food channels are absolutely amazing. Most coffee shops serve some type of pastry, and most pastry shops serve coffee or tea. Few people can resist a well-crafted baked good.

One of these irresistible treats is on the island of Molokai in Hawaii. The Kanemitsu Bakery has a normal storefront and entrance by day, but on Friday and Saturday nights after 8:00 PM there is a back door opening for the purchase of Molokai hot bread that is known by the locals. If you are a "haole" (foreigner) and are fortunate or brave enough to attempt this clandestine mission, you can be seen trading cash **only** in the back alley for this fresh-from-the-oven treat. It is a sweet round of white bread, served piping hot, and slathered with your choice of fillings. Most people start with butter or cream cheese, then they add a fruit filling or cinnamon-sugar mixture that literally melts in your mouth. It is big enough to feed four, and it seldom disappoints the taste buds. As you are awaiting your prize, the smell of the fresh baked bread wafts through the air, making the anticipated delicacy all the more rewarding when it is finally presented.

My brother-in-law, Don, would most definitely be a regular at the Kanemitsu Bakery if he lived anywhere near it. He has always LOVED a good pastry. I believe he has the best bakeries scoped out between Bakersfield, California, and Bend, Oregon. He made the trek from his home in Bakersfield to his wife's hometown in Bend many times throughout their courtship. We often benefited from his fetish as he would bring a chocolate dipped coconut macaroon or an éclair to share with us on his return home.

One of his bakery discoveries is in Turlock, California. It is called Olde Tyme Pastries. We had an opportunity to rendezvous there on a Saturday in February. The minute we walked in, the sweet aromas filled our senses. Among many things in the display cases were German chocolate cakes, caramel covered apple buns, walnut baklava, bear claws, and a variety of pies and cupcakes. The homemade breads were packaged and ready for purchase. I think we gained a few pounds through our senses just by entering the establishment.

On this particular weekend we were meeting up with some relatives who live in Turlock. They had no trouble finding us since this is a well-known bakery in the area. Our sweet cousins, Janice and Darryl, arrived and treated us all to an afternoon latte. Don (of course) purchased a few sweet treats to share amongst us. What a blessing to connect with family in such a way. We spent time sharing our **common ground** through photos, reminiscing about past reunions, and hoping for future ones.

Before we departed, Darryl made a point to ask us if we had any prayer requests. The conversation instantly became deeper as we shared some of our more intense needs. He then prayed for all of us. As we held hands in this bakery, as customers came and went with their pastry and bread purchases, we were reaching out to the Bread of Life.

I don't know if anyone saw us holding hands around the table together and bowing our heads. Maybe a believer saw us and was encouraged in the Lord. Maybe someone looked on and thought we were a little crazy. What I do know is that God meets us anywhere, any time. His "bakery" is open 24/7.

Knowing that the Bread of Life dwells within me, I began to reflect on what my "bakery" looks like to others. Does my life offer a pleasing and sweet aroma to the saved and the perishing? Not to mix analogies too much, but I wondered, is the fruit of the spirit (see Galatians 5:22-23) manifested in my day-to-day words and actions? Here is what I want to be able to offer those around me:

- A slice (or a "*peace*") of pie
- Rolls, hot from the oven, that emanate warmth, welcome and comfort, kneaded with *gentleness*
- Sweet cakes of *goodness* and *kindness*
- Cookies baked with *patience*, offered with *love* and *faithfulness*
- Pastries filled with the *joy* of His presence
- Goodies seasoned and spiced with the *self-control* of my words and attitudes

My prayer is that I can offer these treats straight from the heart of God, to a world that is hungering. They long for more than a slice of Heaven. They yearn for the life-sustaining Bread of Life. What does your display of baked goods look like? What aroma emanates from your life?

 ## Single-Cup Summary

- Bread has significance throughout history, and it is used symbolically in Scripture.
- As the sweet aroma of fresh baked goods is pleasing, we should strive to make our lives a pleasing aroma to the world around us.
- Keeping in step with the Spirit helps us bear life-producing fruit.

Grounded in the Word

- 2 Corinthians 2:15
- Exodus 23:15
- Deuteronomy 8:3
- Matthew 4:1-4
- Matthew 6:9-13
- John 6:35
- 1 Corinthians 11:23-26
- Galatians 5:22-23

Points to Ponder and Percolate

_____

_____

_____

_____

_____

_____

_____

_____

_____

_____

_____

_____

_____

_____

_____

_____

_____

_____

_____

_____

_____

_____

_____

_____

TWO ARE BETTER THAN ONE

Two are better than one...A cord of three strands is not quickly broken. Ecclesiastes 4:9a, 12b

What is better than one cup of coffee? Two cups of coffee, of course. Why? Because that most likely means you are sharing it with someone. When you share a cup of coffee, a meal, a job, or a task with someone else, the assignment tends to get done more efficiently and the experience is much more enjoyable. When a burden weighs you down, it becomes lighter and more bearable when you share it with a friend. Where two or three come together in Jesus' name, He will be with them (see Matthew 18:20).

The bottom line is that two are better than one. When Jesus becomes the third member of the cord, it becomes powerful! We do not thrive when we go through life as a single strand. First, we need to attend to our relationship with Jesus, and second, we must strive to develop relationships that will strengthen us further.

My dad has an identical twin brother. They both played the violin and piano. They both drank their coffee strong and black. They each became a pastor and attended seminary at the same time. Their early pastorates were driving distance apart, and they spent many a Monday together after preaching a Sunday morning and evening sermon. They married sisters, which created an even tighter family bond. Because of our "double cousin" status, all of us kids from both sides of the family did just about everything together. We were often confused as siblings rather than cousins.

Even into retirement years, dad and mom, my Uncle Richard and Aunt Becky, took many road trips together. The car was always a place of perfect harmony. Well,mostly harmony. Like typical siblings they cultivated a competitive spirit, but a day without communicating by phone or email was a very rare occasion.

Maybe because they knew and understood the value of a close bond with someone else, both of these twins valued relationships. My dad took a daily five to ten mile walk in San Diego, often strolling the Pacific Beach Boardwalk. On the way he would see people who routinely walked or sat along the same path. What would begin with a smile and a nod, often turned into a brief chat. That conversation would develop into many more dialogs and discussions, as well as a few visits to the coffee shop. Dad would listen to them, share with them, laugh with them, and pray with them.

Not everyone he encountered had the same faith that he did. One such friend was named Richard. We'll call him Beach Richard so as not to confuse him with his brother, Richard. Often Beach Richard would be sitting on the beach wall waiting for my dad to come by. My dad was concerned for him because he claimed to be an atheist. That didn't stop their encounters and exchanges together or my dad's prayers for him.

Besides love for a hearty walk and a strong cup of coffee, my dad had what he explained as *Adventures with Angels and Accounts of*

Change, the title of a book he wrote. On his walks he would almost always find coins—sometimes a penny, other times multiple amounts. He would pick up these copper and silver pieces and consider them as special attention from the angels, who were playfully acknowledging that they were watching over him. He began to see the coins as more than coincidence or luck, but as an opportunity to thank God for the blessings in his life. He would also pray for blessings in the lives of others.

One day, after meeting with Beach Richard over coffee, they went on their separate ways. My dad almost immediately found a shiny penny. He asked God to help Beach Richard through his perplexing mazes and prayed for an upcoming surgery. When their paths crossed again, dad spoke love and encouragement into his life. He showed him the penny he had found and told him that he had prayed for him. Beach Richard was genuinely touched and thanked him for the blessing.

After my dad passed away from cancer in 2011, my mom made a point to contact Beach Richard and meet with him. Beach Richard responded favorably to her phone call, and they met at Starbucks. It was a beautiful sunny day, and they shared about the weather and a few other mundane things. My mom's purpose was to let Beach Richard know how my dad had been concerned about his spiritual status. She left the meeting greatly relieved because Beach Richard told her he was seriously thinking about God. He attributed this openness to God to my dad, who had treated him with such kindness and respect. My mom again called Beach Richard on his 89th birthday. He reiterated that he had been thinking about God. The blessings of the coins and the coffee had greatly impacted his life. Beach Richard, who otherwise would have remained closed off to thoughts of God, was the beneficiary of not going through life as a single strand!

My mom also shared with me one of her most recent coffee accounts. She had received a gift card to a bagel shop. Not wanting to use it alone, the gift card had stayed in her wallet for quite a long time. One day she called a friend to join her for a coffee and bagel. They met and spent about two hours together sipping coffee. They ended up having one of those precious friend moments when surface communicating becomes deep and heartfelt. As she left that sacred spot, she realized, "Oh my goodness, I didn't know I would be sharing such precious thoughts buried deep within my heart." She felt uplifted as they parted. The cords of their friendship and their relationship with God was something that strengthened her when she didn't even know she had needed it!

And then there's my Uncle Richard. He has expressed many times how he misses his twin! However, that doesn't keep him from developing and nurturing his own relationships. He delights in a daily Caramel Macchiato at a Starbucks near his home in Oceano, California. The baristas know him by name and have his crafted drink ready practically before he gets out of his car. They show concern when he doesn't show up, and they let him know they miss him when he's not there.

Whoever is at the register on any given day knows that Richard will want his receipt. He doesn't need to check the calculations, but he uses the back of the receipt for a very unique purpose. As he begins a quiet time of prayer, he starts out with praise to God, writing in his own spiritual shorthand. He just puts the first letter of each word: **B**lessing, **H**onor, **G**lory, **P**ower, **P**raise, **T**hanksgiving. He thanks God the **F**ather, the **H**oly **S**pirit, and **S**avior **J**esus. He then prays for all kinds of people. Again he writes just initials rather than names as he goes through his litany of kids, grandkids, great grandkids, nieces, nephews, acquaintances, and dear friends. By the time he finishes, the back of the receipt is completely covered with the ink renderings of his prayers. He will sometimes pocket the receipt. Other times he throws it away. If you ever find a strange receipt with what appears to be some type of secret code on the back, you will know that a great saint of the Lord has been praying.

As Uncle Richard sips his coffee and contemplates his prayers and blessings, he has also had opportunities to meet people. Sometimes a stranger will approach him. He will talk with them and occasionally invite them to church. He prays for them if they have a special need. They sense the strength and encouragement that comes from having someone who cares! Other times he has a pre-arranged meeting with a friend or pastor from the area who may just need that special time of fellowship with another Christ follower. Either way, who can do life by themselves?

God knew how much we would need each other. He has placed special people in your life who minister to you at times. He has placed those in your path that you can encourage. Don't do life alone! First and foremost, if you don't know Him, Jesus wants to be by your side every step of the way. When you enter a relationship with Him, humbly confessing your sins and shortcomings, He forgives your sins and helps you to become the best version of yourself, the one He created you to be. Second, reach out to someone. Share some **common ground** through the special touch that comes from a friendly smile or word of support. Meet over a cup of coffee. Maybe you are the one who will be refreshed by the mutual sharing of your heart with someone else. Regardless of whether you are the blessing or the blessed, two are better than one!

 Single-Cup Summary

- Burdens are easier to bear when shared with a friend.
- Value relationships...don't do life alone.
- Accepting Jesus's forgiveness begins your relationship with Him, the Great Burden Taker.
- Lifting your burdens to Jesus in prayer with another believing Christian will complete the cord of three.

 Grounded in the Word

- Ecclesiastes 4:9-12
- Matthew 18:19-20
- Romans 6:23
- Galatians 6:2
- 1 Thessalonians 5:11

Points to Ponder and Percolate

A SAFE PASSAGEWAY

His faithfulness will be your shield and rampart. Psalm 91:4b

In Historic Downtown Bend, Oregon, there is a fun little coffee shop called the Looney Bean. They roast their own coffee locally, and it is superb! You get your cup with a little design created in foam. They advertise that they are "the taste of good times," offering delicious pastries as well as breakfast and lunch items, all from local vendors. This quaint cabin-like structure covered in wooden shingles gives you the feeling that you are in a mountain retreat. It sits on the banks of the Deschutes River overlooking Mirror Pond.

Mirror Pond is an impoundment along the Deschutes River between Pacific Power's Bend Hydro Dam and the Colorado Dam. The area was created by the local parks and recreation district to provide **safe passage** for tubers and kayakers. Drake Park, nearby, has paved walking and biking paths that follow this portion of the river. Ducks and geese are prolific, as well as other wildlife. Great horned owls have taken residence in the trees. In May, when the owlets are born, they receive protection from the public via a temporary fenced-in area. There is a bridge, known as the Galveston Bridge, which spans the water and makes for an idyllic setting.

It was on this bridge that I called my mom. I had just had a divine appointment with two strangers in the Looney Bean, and I could hardly wait to share the story with my prayer partner and confidante. You see, my mom and I, along with many other faithful warriors, had been praying for our son, Jeran, for a couple of decades now. God had been working in me to build my trust and character through these years.

On Father's Day 2004 I had a dream that centered around Hebrews 12. Our son was running a race, and he was surrounded by a crowd of people who loved him and were cheering him on. As the race began, he kept falling until he was lying face down on the track in a pool of blood. Jesus was standing over him. When Jeran asked why this was happening to him and why he was bleeding, Jesus answered that it was not Jeran's blood but that it was Jesus's blood that had been shed for him. I awoke from that dream with my pillow covered in tears. It was an assurance to me that God was not finished with him yet. When I wrote down the story and shared it with Jeran, he told me that someday I would be writing another chapter. This is not the final chapter, but it is the next episode of his story.

The two women we met in the Looney Bean were fellow believers. I'm not even sure how our conversation began, but it became apparent early on that they shared our faith and relationship with Jesus, the Savior. One of the women shared about a job change she was going to be experiencing soon which would move her to the Paso Robles, California, area. My husband's family grew up around there, so there was an immediate connection. Her job would be to develop a health and counseling program for those trapped in addictions. The goal was to help clients to be able to pinpoint the root causes of their problem. She planned to infuse the program with spiritual truth so that they could find freedom from their chains of bondage.

I ended up sharing with them about our son, who deals with addictions. I had been experiencing a season of doubt, almost to the point of despair, because of his recent poor choices. In May of 2017, my mom had been at a retreat where she received anointing and healing on behalf of Jeran. She was certain that God was doing a work on our son. This was a time when I needed someone to fill in the gap for me. I did not seem to have the words to say or the faith to say them. I knew Jesus was my intercessor, but I also needed others to help lift me up in faith. In Exodus 17, the Israelites only prevailed over the Amalekites when Aaron and Hur helped lift the weary arms of Moses. My mom had been my Aaron. Now I was meeting my Hur.

On this day in September of 2017, the prayer these ladies prayed for my son was straight from the heart of God. They claimed Psalm 91 over his life. The Holy Spirit prompted them to pray for things in his life that I had not even shared with them. My tears flowed, and my heart overflowed, with the goodness of God. The promises from the scripture were for me as much as for my son. I recognized that the Lord is my refuge and my fortress. I didn't need to fear or despair because his faithfulness would be my shield and rampart. I felt a burden lift from my heart that had been subtly robbing me of my joy.

The name of one of the women was Joy Victor. It sounded like something straight out of *Pilgrim's Progress*. This meeting was not a coincidence but a divine appointment. She was placed in my path to help me once again claim victory against Satan's wiles and schemes. She later told me that when she walked by our table to order her coffee, she sensed that God was present and ready to move. She wasn't surprised when she returned with her order and found that we had struck up a conversation with her friend.

Like Mirror Pond and the safe passage, God has provided His safety net around His beloved. There may be moments of dangerous rapids and frightening capsizings, but God will be our shield and rampart! As we all are, our son is a work in progress. With renewed faith we will keep praying for his complete healing, freedom, and for safety as he navigates down life's river.

We all go through times of trial! Think about who might need you to stand in the gap for them. Maybe someone is lifting your weary arms right now. Whatever the case, listen to God's call. You might be asked by Him to lift the burden of a complete stranger. Or He might send someone your way that shares **common ground** and can encourage your soul. His ramparts are providing a **safe passageway!**

 ## Single-Cup Summary

- We need to stand in the gap in prayer for each other.
- Just as Moses needed Aaron and Hur to help raise his weary arms for victory in battle, we sometimes need others to lift us when we are weary in our spiritual warfare.
- Using scripture verses is a powerful way to pray.

Grounded in the Word

- Psalm 91
- Hebrews 12:1-13
- Exodus 17:8-13
- Esther 4:12-17

Points to Ponder and Percolate

YOUR HEART'S DESIRE

Delight yourself in the Lord, and he will give you the desires of your heart. Psalm 37:4

I recently had the honor of talking to Morgan (Burnard) Bonn about her coffee journey. She currently owns and operates Cloud 9 Coffee Company. As we were sharing about God giving us the desires of our heart, Morgan made this profound statement about how God works. "It is typically never the way I think it's going to happen, but it always works out, and I'm always thankful for it."

Morgan started her company at the age of twenty-two, but God had put the dream and desire in her heart many years earlier. She shared with me that even as a child the Lord had instilled in her an entrepreneurial spirit. She loved thinking of ways she could sell something to make money, and knew in her heart that someday she would do something great. During her sophomore year at Point Loma Nazarene University in San Diego, California, Morgan began dreaming about a brick and mortar coffee shop that she could start in her home town. She was struck by the amazing coffee culture in San Diego, and she wanted to be able to start something similar in Bakersfield, one mug at a time.

"Coffee culture," I thought to myself. "What is she talking about?" Coffee Culture in America is defined as "a social atmosphere or series of associated social behaviors that depends heavily upon coffee, particularly as a social lubricant." According to a 2011 *Scientific American* article, in the 1970's and 80's coffee companies had to wake up to the realization that twenty to twenty-nine-year-olds associated coffee with their parents and grandparents. They were losing ground on a new coffee generation. On top of that, the prices of the bland and weak coffee products they were offering were rising because of the frost in Brazil in 1975. Over the next few decades they realized they needed to make coffees more personable and accessible. They brought along the twenty-somethings into the coffee culture by appealing to the "me" generation. Now there was a flavor for everyone, a coffee for every lifestyle. Where and how the coffee beans were produced and traded became very important as well. Over time coffee was revitalized to be that drink over which people could socialize or receive a mid-day productivity boost.[2]

So Morgan's dream to help socially lubricate Bakersfield through a stellar cup of coffee began. During the summer before her senior year at Point Loma, Morgan attended coffee school. Morgan explained how she learned the ins and outs of a coffee business, as well as details about growing, harvesting, and roasting coffee beans. She earned her "coffee degree," and used her new knowledge to develop a business plan. She had done all the market research and was figuring out how to make it work. The start-up costs were about $500,000, so Morgan began talking to potential investors. After meeting with several people, the dream looked like it was fading. Most everyone felt like it was too high a risk to put

---

[2] D'Costa, Krystal. "The Culture of Coffee Drinkers." <u>Scientific American</u>. 11 August 2011 <https://blogs.scientificamerican.com/anthropology-in-practice/the-culture-of-coffee-drinkers/>

that much money in to someone with zero experience in the coffee industry.

Morgan returned to her last semester of college discouraged, disappointed, and a little bit depressed. She didn't want to graduate with her Political Science degree and her God-birthed vision of the coffee house, just to live with her parents. It's not that she didn't love her parents, it just wasn't part of **her** goals for her future. God had not forgotten her! He was getting ready to give her the desire of her heart in His way and in His time. Morgan admitted she had been relying on her own strengths and abilities to make things happen, asking God to help her efforts along the way. God, however, knew what was best for her, and He began to close doors so others could open. He brought her to a point of putting her reliance fully on Him!

A new door was about to open. Mid-semester she received a call from a friend from coffee school who had purchased a tiny little trailer which she had converted into a mobile coffee shop. Even after seeing some pictures, Morgan kind of passed it off as a little bit of a weird idea. Not too long afterward, Morgan was at a family gathering on the East Coast. She was telling her family about what her friend was doing. It had moved from being a "weird" idea to an "interesting" idea. They began discussing the possibilities and realized it was actually a viable idea. First and foremost, it wasn't a $500,000 venture.

Morgan contacted the guy who had converted her friend's trailer. After pitching her vision to see if it was even possible to create the type of a space she imagined, the ball started rolling. The gentleman who would be converting the unit was as excited about the project as Morgan and her family. She almost immediately found her funding source. Along the way, her dad became her business partner. They wanted Cloud 9 to be unique, so they worked on the mission statement and goals together. They wanted to be relational, putting people over profit. They wanted to be able to invest in the community through service projects and by helping non-profit organizations. They articulated their priorities for the business and discussed how to stick to those goals going forward.

April 1, 2017, was opening day. Morgan shared that their customers are the best people in the world. She said that the people they meet are sent from God. Events they do and people they serve have worked together for His ultimate purpose. It is an indicator that God is in control and that she couldn't have orchestrated any of this on her own. Most of the time it's the little things that become something more. A friend of a friend of her mom recommended Cloud 9 for a bridal shower. Since the shower, this lady has booked Cloud 9 for multiple events at her house as well as at the couple's business. The relationships with the people who sell their local wares in front of their coffee unit have proven to be very beneficial to each other. Meeting people at different events has opened up contacts that she would not have otherwise had, that could potentially be part of God's plan for a future career in Political Science. The story is still being written!

For now, the plan is to continue expanding Cloud 9 Coffee Company. They have purchased an additional bus to place somewhere on the west side of town. Morgan still dreams of having a brick and mortar location someday, but right now being mobile is a plus for them. They can create **common ground** anywhere. They are able to do customer or employee appreciation events at local businesses, receptions, showers, weddings, and community events like the Third Thursday in downtown Bakersfield. They serve coffee at fund raisers like the Links for Life. The one down side is moving the trailer. Everything has to be battened down so that it doesn't fly around in transit. Hitching the trailer to her truck, in Morgan's words, is horrible! She smiles as she says it just gives her one more opportunity to display her independence as a businesswoman.

As we finished the conversation about the business, it naturally segued into another God-thing that has been the desire of Morgan's heart for a long time. Morgan had prayed for her future spouse from the time she was a young girl, and she had recently become engaged. Morgan met her future husband, Carter, through a Christian dating website. She rolled her eyes as she spoke, knowing the sometimes poor and verifiable reputation of such ventures. When we wait patiently for God and trust in Him, He can work through any avenue! Morgan had experienced previous relationships that she knew were not "the one." At a time of feeling a bit hopeless that she would find that special someone, she read Carter's profile. His opinions about certain topics led her to message him.

What started as a need to set him straight on some issues, morphed into some great conversations and deep dialogues about life and their relationships with Christ. From there they began to talk more and more. She saw how Carter loved the Lord in such a genuine way. He, too, had prayed for his future spouse since he was fourteen or so. They began dating and getting to know each other better. In a very romantic move, Carter planned a photo shoot by a mutual friend in a forest area around Frasier Park. He and the photographer had a secret word that would indicate that it was the perfect lighting and setting for the engagement to be recorded. Morgan was totally oblivious to what was about to happen, but when she saw Carter on one knee, she joyfully said YES!

God's timing and ways are perfect! Things typically don't happen the way we think they are going to happen. He usually has work to do in us in order to make sure we are growing into the person He wants us to be. Psalm 37 can be a great comfort and fits so aptly to Morgan's story. We sometimes get angry with God for not giving us what our hearts desire, but He wants us to trust Him (vs. 4), commit our way to Him (vs. 5), be still before Him and wait patiently for Him (vs. 7). When we get to our lowest point and realize we can only depend on Him, we begin to see the desires of our heart (vs. 4). He will make our righteous reward shine like the dawn (vs. 6). The dawn is definitely shining through Cloud 9!

 ## Single-Cup Summary

- God typically accomplishes His plans for our lives in a way that is different from what we expect, but it is always good.
- God's ways and thoughts are higher than our ways.
- God-birthed ideas come to fruition in His timing.

 ## Grounded in the Word

- Psalm 37:3-7
- Isaiah 55:8-9
- 2 Peter 3:8-9

Points to Ponder and Percolate

LOVE IS IN THE AIR

Let us rejoice and be glad and give him glory! For the wedding of the Lamb has come, and his bride has made herself ready.
Revelation 19:7

Since my husband and I do not drink alcohol, it was a pleasant surprise to have an open coffee bar at a wedding we attended last summer. The mobile unit that was hired to serve coffee and tea drinks was none other than Cloud 9 Coffee Company. Although it was an outdoor wedding in Bakersfield, with a balmy temperature of ninety-seven degrees, we were able to order some iced coffee drinks that were very refreshing. For that matter, there's no better place than a wedding and a wedding feast to share **common ground** with people you might not normally see that often. Back in the old days, when we got married, we stuck to cake and punch receptions. It was a super fancy wedding if hors d'oeuvres were served! Today's couples have a full sit-down dinner for all of their guests. I think I'm glad we had three boys!!!

A few summers ago, our family had several of these joyous celebrations. I remember the call from my dad. "I do believe love is in the air," he chuckled over the phone. The romantic that he is, he had called us immediately to tell us about the engagement of my nephew, Rob. Dad was certain that love was flowing through our family and permeating the air, and he predicted we might hear of a couple more engagements before too long. Sure enough, we ended up with three weddings that summer.

My sister's son, Rob, was the first to propose. His engagement to Jessica was quite the thriller. He had arranged for a picnic dinner to be delivered and served by friends on the beach. At the end of their meal, Rob pulled out a poem he had written to Jessica, which ended in asking for her hand in marriage. She accepted, of course. Then they were whisked away to Coronado Island's Hotel Del Coronado where, to Jessica's complete surprise, both his family and her family were there to greet and congratulate them. They enjoyed a scrumptious dessert in the luxurious dining area. As the evening ended, fireworks burst over the harbor. When you hear my dad tell about it, you would have thought the fireworks display was planned just for the engaged couple, but it certainly did enhance the romance of the evening.

A few months later our son was engaged. He also elaborately planned the evening, starting with a special dinner. The couple ended back at his apartment, where his pastor and wife had snuck in and provided a romantic setting with rose petals and candle light for the moment when he proposed. They were hiding with cameras in hand to capture the moments after she said "yes."

Young love is so impressive. I love to watch the eyes of the couple—they say it all. There is a look of admiration, trust, and a longing to know the person completely. There is a look of contentment, joy, and dedication. We so enjoyed watching the eyes of our son and his bride on their wedding day. In spite of the hustle and bustle of the pictures, the one hundred two degree heat of the afternoon, and the anxious anticipation that all would go well, when the wedding song was played, all else fell by the wayside. As

Kate walked down the aisle, her eyes locked on Jeff's eyes. There was such love flowing between them, we all wanted to get married all over again. It was precious, contagious, and comforting, all at once. You were certain that they truly meant their vows, that they were really saying these things for life. They were sealing the commitment that they had made in their hearts with words before a crowd of witnesses.

The week before Jeff and Kate's wedding, we attended a week long family camp meeting in the Sierras. Our speaker, Dr. Dan Spaite, an ER doctor who uses his medical knowledge to draw parallels to the Christian life, spoke one evening on how the church has lost its first love. We don't have the Bridegroom's return constantly on our minds. We have allowed other loves to push Him to the back of our thoughts instead of keeping His coming again at the forefront of our minds. Dr. Spaite reminded us that the true bride is made up of those who are so deeply in love with the Bridegroom that they can't wait for the wedding day.

I was deeply moved to keep the fire of the Spirit alive in my life and to wait in readiness and anticipation for His coming. I was challenged to nurture my relationship with Jesus and make Him the primary focus of every aspect of my life. Dr. Spaite taught how the Christian attitude of watching for Christ's return indicates awaiting eagerly, looking and waiting for him, dressed in readiness. The analogy to the events that were about to take place in our family provided a great context for understanding my role in my relationship to Jesus and his second coming.

Kate couldn't wait for her wedding day. She had the beautiful white gown which symbolized their commitment to each other to remain sexually pure and faithful to one another. Her bridesmaids were helping her get the perfect hair style and jewels. The couple had the impeccable rings engraved with their love for each other. She had no question that Jeff adored her, and her admiration for him was reciprocated. They talked daily before the wedding declaring their love for each other. All of the planning and preparation was based on a deep relationship.

And so it is with us. As the bride of Christ looks forward to the great wedding day with adoration toward the Bridegroom, it comes out of a response to His love for her. He has provided a beautiful garment of white without spot or wrinkle which was bought at the ultimate price. She is bedecked with jewels of strength and joy. She is engraved in the palms of His hand—never forgotten. He adores her. He has written a letter to her so she will always know of His love for her. He is faithful to her and will provide for her best interests.

So encourage each other with these words. "According to the Lord's own word, we tell you that we who are still alive, who are left till the coming of the Lord, will certainly not precede those who have fallen asleep. For the Lord Himself will come down from heaven, with a loud command, with the voice of the archangel and with the trumpet call of God, and the dead in Christ will rise first. After that, we who are still alive and are left will be caught up together with them in the clouds to meet the Lord in the air. And so we will be with the Lord forever" (1 Thessalonians 4:15-17).

My dad was right. Love was in the air, and he traveled many a mile that summer to help everyone celebrate. And someday He who **is** Love will be **in the air** to take us home with Him forever.

Single-Cup Summary

- As the bride of Christ, we should be so deeply in love with the Bridegroom that we can't wait for the wedding day.
- We need to be eagerly looking and waiting for Christ's second coming, dressed in readiness.
- Someday Christ will be in the air to take us home with Him forever.

 ## Grounded in the Word

- Revelation 19:7-9
- Isaiah 49:16
- 1 Thessalonians 4:15-17

Points to Ponder and Percolate

HOT COFFEE

So, because you are lukewarm—neither hot nor cold—I am about to spit you out of my mouth. Revelation 3:16

My mother-in-law is a precious woman! She is ninety-three years old and as cute as ever. She likes to "take" us to lunch, so we pick her up and drive her to whatever restaurant she has a hankering for at that moment. The other day we were at a local coffee shop. We had been grocery shopping previously and she had picked up some small Christmas bows to put on top of some homemade goodies she was making for the neighbors. She pulled the bows out of her purse and stuck them on all of our foreheads. We took a selfie and had a good laugh.

Another time when we were out and about, she spotted a bright red 1964 Cadillac convertible in the parking lot. It was in prime condition. She asked me to take her picture standing next to it. I looked around, a little embarrassed since I didn't know who the owner was. I wasn't sure if he would approve of us stalking his beautifully restored car. As I reluctantly finished a couple of shots of her standing next to the car, the owner and his family came out of the restaurant. They were thrilled that she showed such an interest, and the owner even let her sit in the driver's seat for a couple more photo ops.

As her memory is beginning to fade with her years, there is one thing we all agree upon—her spirit has remained happy and sweet.

For every meal we fix for her, every visit we pay her, every errand we run for her, she gushes over us. According to her, we are the most precious, loving people on the planet! When she bites into a meal we have prepared, no matter how simple, she raves about the freshness and flavor. Through the years my sisters-in-law and I have laughed over the fact that she has told us each, at separate times, that our chicken noodle soup or our cookies are the BEST she has ever tasted!

There are a couple of things, however, about which she will not compromise! One of those things is her prayer life. She has a unique and sweet relationship with the Lord. She keeps a prayer board that is filled with so many chalked in names and requests, that you can barely see any chalkboard through the writing. When sleep eludes her at night, she meets with the Holy Spirit and prays over all of her kids, grandkids, and great grandkids. Besides her immediate family, she is "Grandma" to many in the church. She calls out to God for their lives and problems as well.

The other thing she will not compromise is the temperature of her coffee. When we are ordering our drinks at a restaurant, she will ask for a cup of decaf. She will add with emphasis, "It needs to be HOT!" If the server brings the coffee and it is not to her preference, she will send it back for a reheat. Most of the waiters and waitresses who have served our table in the past will remember her request, and they will make a fresh pot of decaf just for her. That usually ensures that the cup will be steaming hot and palatable to her.

She has never spit or spewed the coffee, but I have seen her make a pretty disgusted face if it is not right! Coffee and tea are just made to be consumed either ice cold or piping hot. Lukewarm does not cut it! And so it is with our Christian walk. Jesus made it clear that we are not to be fence sitters. We are not to be lukewarm. Because we are neither hot nor cold, He is about to spew us out of His mouth. Another translation says He is about to vomit us out of His mouth. That is a pretty violent depiction of His concern for our spiritual temperature!

In this same passage, Jesus goes on to say, "You say, 'I am rich; I have acquired wealth and do not need a thing.' But you do not realize that you are wretched, pitiful, poor, blind, and naked" (Revelation 3:17). He goes on to encourage and counsel us to "buy" from Him the type of gold that is refined in the fire that will make us spiritually wealthy. He offers us "white clothes" of His salvation, the only thing that will cover the shame of our sin. He provides salve for our eyes so that we may be healed from our spiritual blindness.

We are in a dangerous place in our culture of having a misplaced self-reliance. We take pride in what we have accomplished, and we can so easily get caught up in the fact that we don't need anything. Just take a look at all the "stuff" we have sitting around in our closets. When we begin to feel satisfied with what we've done for ourselves, we become in even greater danger of forgetting our wretchedness and our need for our Redeemer and Lord. Our love for God can become lukewarm. We think we have the best of both worlds, when in reality we are seriously lacking spiritual depth and the richness that God wants for our lives.

The next time you order your coffee, consider ordering it extra hot. Let it remind you to fan the flame of your fire for God. As you share with others over **common ground**, intensify the heat of your concern for the status of your hearts. As you walk through life be

God-confident, not self-confident. Place Him at the center of each problem, each victory, each relationship, and each daily task. Guard your heart from complacency by spending daily time meditating on God's word. Ask God to help show you areas of pride and independence in your life that you need to change to praise and dependence on Him. Turn up the heat in your relationship! Be on fire for God! He likes it HOT!

 ## Single-Cup Summary

- We should not compromise our prayer life.
- The Christian life is not for fence-sitters.
- We need to guard against prideful complacency.
- To keep on fire for God, we must fan the flame of our spiritual walk daily.

 ## Grounded in the Word

- Philippians 4:6-7
- Revelation 3:14-18
- 2 Timothy 1:6-7

 *Points to Ponder and Percolate*

MAYOR BOB

So neither he who plants nor he who waters is anything, but only God, who makes things grow. I Corinthians 3:7

The Starbucks closest to my house is on a street called Coffee Road. How fun is that? I'm not sure of the origin of the road's name, but I imagined how it might have been labeled.

Before we moved into our neighborhood, and even for several years after, we were surrounded by orchards. The thoroughfare past our boys' high school dead ended at a canal. We had to drive to hi-ways and bi-ways either north or south in order to eventually continue in a westward direction. With all of the surrounding agriculture, I'm sure that during the early morning hours, field hands and farmers gathered to begin the work of planting or harvesting crops. Perhaps Coffee Road was the route by which the foreman sent the water and coffee trucks to fuel the workers for the day. Maybe before the road was named, people looked forward to the coffee run and anxiously peered down the way to see if the truck was getting close. Perhaps they took their mid-morning coffee and water breaks close to the road and shared about work, their families, their futures and dreams. They met on **common ground** over common grounds of coffee to share and build relationships.

Another possibility is that truckers recognized Coffee Road as a good back road to eventually get to the main highway. You could hear the air brakes and gears shifting as they traveled down the road late at night, or early in the morning. Maybe the truck drivers knew that the sleep that threatened to overtake them as they continued their route would soon be thwarted and caffeinated at a truck stop not too far down the road. Just the thought of soon getting a cup of hot coffee to-go kept them motivated and awake along this route.

Whatever the origin of Coffee Road's name, I still love that my local coffee hang-out is on this road! I'm also privileged to have a friend named Bob, whom my friends and I have endearingly dubbed "Mayor" of the Coffee Road Starbucks. On any given day, at any given time in the morning or afternoon, you can walk in and see "Mayor Bob" enjoying the Starbucks community. He greets people as they come in, and he will often break away from the group he is talking with to find out how someone is doing. He knows the staff by name, and of course, they know his name and drink of choice. For the past 12 years he has met regularly with a group of men from all walks of life who shoot the breeze and work at solving the world's problems.

Not everyone has the time and opportunity to make this a daily routine, but we all can seek creative ways to connect with others. Bob is fortunate to have a business out of his home that allows him to break away for periods of time. He uses the time at Starbucks for networking, communicating, and ministering. I asked him to share some of his **common ground** moments. Here are a couple of his accounts.

One of the men who frequented the group was an avowed atheist. For the sake of privacy, we'll call him Fred. Fred had a background that caused him great hurt and hatred of the church. His father had "punished" him by sending Fred and his siblings to church to give himself a break from the kids. Fred's picture of God the Father, who is nothing but good, was tainted and poisoned by his earthly father who did not understand how to love and guide his own children. Fred would enter into conversations with the Starbuck's group and was often cantankerous, trying to trap and convince the others of their foolhardy ways spiritually, politically, and emotionally.

At times it was wearing, but the group, and especially Bob, made sure Fred knew he was accepted and loved. After a while, Fred decided that he needed a different group of men who were more like-minded, so he began going to a different Starbucks. Every once in a while, Bob would run into him, and he found out that Fred had been facing a very devastating medical issue. Bob took the matter to prayer and took the situation to the Coffee Road group. Together they helped to raise some money for his medical expenses. They believed that they might be the only "Jesus" Fred would see in his life. The seed of love was planted. It is up to God to find those to water and harvest, but God is in the process of growing this act of love into a tree of righteousness someday.

Another story centered around one of the baristas. As mentioned, Bob knew the staff by name and made it a point to show genuine interest in their lives. One in particular, we'll call Tracy, was a college student who loved animals. Bob and his wife were able to use her to care for their pets on several occasions while they were out of town. She grew to love the animals, and she knew there was something special about their "parents." Consequently, when she was getting ready to move to Sacramento to pursue her career and move closer to her boyfriend, she asked to see the pets for one last time.

Bob and his wife recognized the visit as an opportunity to pour love into her life. They not only welcomed her to come see the dogs and cat, but they extended her an invitation to breakfast. Around that sacred meal, they were able to let her know that they would be praying for her. They spoke to her about her relationship with her boyfriend, and encouraged her to be patient for love to grow between them. They shared about how God had worked in their marriage, and how with Him as the center and with hard work and commitment they made it, in spite of all odds. Tracy expressed how grateful she was for the honest and poignant advice. She let them know that no one had ever talked to her about things like this. The seed was planted. Some of the roots of her childhood began to surface, and she headed to Sacramento being more aware of the God who loves and pursues the lost. When she comes back into town, she calls to get together with Bob and his wife. God is at work.

Mayor Bob does not stand on a soap box or pile of coffee beans to share his testimony or condemn others. He lovingly listens, prays and infuses his conversations with a natural salt and light that comes only from one who has a deep personal relationship with the Lord and Savior, Jesus Christ. It may not be for him, or any of us for that matter, to know on this side of heaven the impact we have had on those around us. Our job is not to force our spiritual truths on people, but to live them out before them. When God provides the opportunities, we need to seize them and make sure we are being obedient. Then, He can do His job—making the seeds grow!

Single-Cup Summary

- We can all find creative ways to connect with others.
- Knowing someone's story helps us love through the eyes of Jesus.
- We might be the only "Jesus" others see.
- Letting people into our lives and being vulnerable with them opens the door for God to work.
- It is not our responsibility to condemn or judge, but to be a servant of the tasks God gives to us.
- We need to seize our opportunities to share God's love, and let God do the growing.

 ## Grounded in the Word

- 1 Corinthians 3:5-9
- Matthew 7:1-5
- Hebrews 13:20-21

Points to Ponder and Percolate

_____

_____

_____

_____

_____

_____

_____

_____

_____

_____

_____

_____

_____

_____

_____

_____

_____

_____

_____

_____

_____

ALL GROUND UP

As the heavens are higher than the earth, so are my ways higher than your ways and my thoughts than your thoughts. Isaiah 55:9

The distance from the planet Earth to the heavens is mind-boggling. The moon is 238,900 miles away. It would take about six months to get there if we could drive a car non-stop. It is equivalent to circling the Earth's circumference ten times. To get to Mars, 33.9 million miles away at its closest proximity to our planet, would take a mere 300 days by spacecraft. The nearest stars to the Earth are in the Alpha Centauri system. This triple star system is about 4.37 light-years away. One light-year is 5.9 trillion miles.

Though these distances are incredible to contemplate, these figures are just the tip of the iceberg when we are considering God's ways. His wisdom and power, His methods and timing, and His plans and purposes, are far beyond what we can even begin to concoct. We often begin to think that we have life figured out without God, but then things come crashing in. We lose our way. We flounder in the muck of life. We struggle to get our heads above the water, much less into the heavens. We suffer defeat and misplace our purpose.

We are all made to have purpose in life. It doesn't matter if we feel washed up, used up, dried up, or fed up. It doesn't matter if we feel passed up, passed over, passed by, or passed out. God has us in our circumstances, our position, our location, for a divine reason. Remember that our thoughts are limited to time and space as we know it. God's thoughts and ways are higher than anything we can imagine, and He has had us in His thoughts since before we were conceived. He has a purpose, and a repurpose for each of us.

We do have a choice as to whether or not we allow ourselves to be used by God for His purpose. Choice number one is to grumble and complain that things are not going our way. We are too old, too qualified, too weary, or too busy. We spin our wheels making excuses, wasting precious moments, and throwing away opportunities.

Our second choice is to accept our situation, thank God in the midst of it, and seek how He wants to bring glory to His name. It's hard to be **mad at God** when we recognize we were **made by God**. He has the best in mind for His creation, and He has put us in the right place at the right time, no matter how uncomfortable, unexpected, or unforeseen it seems to be.

Consider your old coffee grounds. Even after you have brewed that perfect pot of coffee, the grounds have a multitude of purposes. Don't throw them away! You can use them in your garden as pest repellent, fertilizer, and compost. You can use them around your house to absorb food odors, as a natural cleaning abrasive, in homemade candles, and to clean out your fireplace. You can use them to exfoliate your skin, to make rejuvenating soap, and to treat your damaged hair. You can even use coffee grounds to create a scrub that will help reduce cellulite!

Ponder those old tea bags. They can be repurposed to flavor your pasta, feed your garden, and clean carpets and rugs. They can be used as deodorizer for your home, deterrent for your household pests, and degreaser for your dirty dishes. You can use tea grounds to soothe, scrub, or soak your tired skin. They can be used to renew wood surfaces, clean glass, and dye paper or cloth.

There are endless amazing methods of reusing what seemed useless. Even more amazing is how God uses what may seem to our human minds as useless. His perfect plan for us often includes discipline and training, trials and pain, suffering and sorrow. When we feel as if we are all ground up with life's realities, God pours His living water over the old **common grounds** of our lives and repurposes his creation!

I have seen it first-hand. I know people who have been through divorce who now help fertilize the soil in the lives of others who are experiencing this lonely time. I know of those who have experienced devastating loss of loved ones through disease or tragedy, who are now a soothing balm to others who are grieving. I have seen lives that seemed to be destroyed by the life of addiction, now helping others to absorb the odors and stench of their former lives. I have watched couples who were redeemed from the pit of sin who now creatively touch the people they meet with the unique flavor of God's Word and His Spirit.

What the world would like to chalk up as "done" or "has been" can and will be new and fresh in the hands of the Almighty God! Play the "what if" game for just a moment:
- What if your prodigal child could come back to God and be used mightily for Him?
- What if your broken relationships could be restored to a better-than-ever love?
- What if your anxiety could be turned into peaceful trust?

- What if the senior citizen could find a new ministry?
- What if your lay-off could open up a new opportunity for your career or develop new relationships with people you were meant to touch?
- What if God could take your sorrow and turn it into joy?
- What if your weakness, given to God, could make you strong?

Enough of the "what ifs!" God can and He will do all of this and more. As the heavens are higher than the earth, His ways are higher than ours. When I contemplate the distance from the earth to the heavens, I can't even fathom it! God's thoughts and dreams for our lives are far above and beyond what we can imagine. Don't give up! Let God take the used up grounds of your life and use it for His glory!

 Single-Cup Summary

- God's ways—His wisdom and power, His methods and timing, His plans and purposes—are far beyond our comprehension.
- When we suffer defeat and misplace our purpose, God is ready to repurpose our lives.
- God has had us in His thoughts since before we were conceived.
- We have a choice: go our own way OR accept God's way.

- His living water will pour over us and well up in us, allowing us to thrive in His eternal life.

 ## Grounded in the Word

- Isaiah 55:9
- Ephesians 3:20-21
- Psalm 139:13-16
- Deuteronomy 30:19-20
- John 4:14

Points to Ponder and Percolate

A CUP OF TEA

"But God demonstrates his love for us in this: While we were still sinners, Christ died for us." Romans 5:8

Some of you are very happy to see a chapter about tea. I know not everyone "gets" coffee. Afternoon tea has surely been a way people have found **common ground**, and there is definitely a place for this British tradition in our developing relationships.

The Romans 5:8 scripture is awe-inspiring. Christ didn't wait until we became what He intended for us to become before He presented Himself as the ultimate sacrifice for our salvation. He died for us "when we were still powerless" (see Romans 5:6). This is so significant! He saw our potential and was willing to stake His life on the possibilities. Paul explains in his letter to the Romans, rarely will a man die for someone righteous, though he might possibly do so if the person is good enough (see Romans 5:7). Yet Christ saved us when we were His enemies so that we could experience an abundant life. Amazing!

As an elementary school teacher, I have thought about this concept a lot as I have dealt with challenging students through the years. I try to think of how God sees them. He died for them, too!

We have a comment code on one of our progress reports that reads: Not working to his/her potential. How can I mark that unless I see the prospects of the student's abilities? And how can I see these prospects except through the eyes of God? I know that my primary goal is to help students reach their academic aptitude. However, I also see my job as a ministry, one that will help students reach their emotional and spiritual capability as well. Finding a way to accomplish this in an already crowded curriculum and schedule is not easy.

The idea of serving tea came as a joint effort of a couple of my Christian colleagues. The first time the seed was planted was the summer of 2002. As we began planning our summer vacation to the northern part of Washington State, it was recommended to us by several sources to take the ferry to Victoria, British Columbia. Coincidentally, one of my fifth grade teaching buddies and her husband were going to be in Victoria at the same exact time.

We decided to rendezvous at the Fairmont Empress Hotel for afternoon tea. Throughout history, this hotel has played host to kings, queens, movie stars and other famous people. It is a five-star hotel, the epitome of elegance. One of its specialties is serving afternoon tea.

Built in 1908, the mid-twentieth century found the hotel looking faded and somewhat dowdy. In 1965 there was a debate on whether to tear it down to make room for a modern, functional high-rise hotel or to refurbish and renew it. The decision was made to restore it to its original stylishness, and what the planners called "Operation Teacup" began. Over the next decade or so, the transformation of this stately hotel would take place.

Years later, we were some of the many recipients of the renovation. In order to partake in the afternoon tea, our reservations had to be made quite a ways in advance. From the minute we walked into the lobby, we felt special. The beautiful craftsmanship that has been preserved, the quiet beauty of every aspect of the building, shouted that this was going to be an extraordinary experience. Then we entered the dining area.

Every item was prepared to perfection and beauty. Each delicate sandwich and pastry was presented in such a way that you knew you were being treated like the kings and queens before you. The servers attended your every need. There was a sense of longing for time to stand still, that the moment would linger just a little longer.

Later we discussed how this would be a unique way to let our students know how much we cared about them. We could set up a little tea party, provide a special invitation, and give a student or two an exquisite experience to enjoy and relish.

The school year started, things got real busy, and the idea of offering tea got pushed aside. Every once in a while we would find ourselves discussing it again, but it never seemed to get off the ground.

In the fall of 2004, another of my fifth grade colleagues shared with me a book she had been reading in which a college professor had taken a group of his failing students to dinner. In sharing over a meal, some of the communication barriers began to break down. The students saw the teacher as someone who was truly interested in them, and the teacher discovered some of the issues that were troubling his students. It made an impact on their lives, and they started performing better in his class as a fringe benefit.

I knew, then and there, that it was high time to start high tea. I went to Walmart, picked up some essential items, and began the next Monday. The students were full of curiosity when they walked in and saw the reading table set with cups and saucers, paper doilies, and napkins. Then they noticed a "private" invitation on two students' desks requesting their presence for tea at the next recess. Their interest was piqued when right before recess I pulled out an electric teapot, filled it with water, and plugged it in.

I never get tired of the process. Students really feel honored when they receive the invitation. Some have never dined in such "elegance," and the expectation for their behavior and manners comes very naturally. They giggle as they are asked for one or two lumps of sugar (I only use sugar cubes). And most important, they open up a side of themselves in which I probably wouldn't otherwise be able to share.

As I recall some of the specific incidents, I am filled with emotion. I have seen some of my hardest students soften. I have seen some of my most needy students revel in the attention. I have seen some of my most insecure students beam with confidence as they share with their friends at recess about their special tea event.

One evening, after a most memorable Monday tea time, I was having trouble sleeping. For some reason my mind kept focusing on a particular student. I remembered how his rather thick fingers had trouble holding the tea cup that was set before him, but he loved the entire experience.

I believe God gave me a little sneak preview into this student's potential. Though the following story is fiction, it represents how this meager sacrifice of my time and effort helps me see my students with fresh eyes. In no way am I intending to glorify my efforts. I am only trying to be an instrument of God, who saw enough potential in **my** humanity to **die for me**.

> *Mike's attention was caught by the whistling of the tea kettle in the kitchen. He had been enjoying the company of his ten-year-old grandson. The two of them were about to embark on an early morning fishing trip, and Mike was fixing them a hot breakfast. There was something about a full stomach, layers of clothing to keep you warm in the chilly spring morning, and a fishing pole that Mike and little Mikey never tired of together.*
>
> *As he placed the scrambled eggs and ham with homemade biscuits and jelly before his little namesake, Mike said a prayer of thankfulness. He then poured the tea. He watched Mikey take the mug in his small, growing hands, clasping its smooth, round surface for warmth. They would be warm soon enough. This day was supposed to be a nice one, and long before noon they would be peeling off their layers.*
>
> *As always, Mikey had asked for two lumps of sugar. He had stared into the cup, mesmerized by the way the sugar cube broke off into smaller pieces, until the crystals completely disappeared into the hot liquid. Each time it seemed as if he were seeing this amazing dissolving process for the first time.*
>
> *Big Mike knew such a contentment in his life. What was it about this simple cup of tea that seemed to evoke a well of emotions and senses in him? His mind wandered back to the first cup of tea he had ever been served. He was a fifth grader, and one Monday morning he received a curious invitation to tea from his math teacher. "You are invited to Room 1 at 9:30 today for tea," the invitation had said. Not really having*

a clue what "tea" meant, he was distracted during all of reading period with his wonderings.

Nine thirty came. The rest of the students went out for their normal recess time. Mike and another student from Room 1 were received by Mrs. Jacobs. The small reading table had been transformed into a decorative place setting for three. Paper doilies lined glass plates. A teapot graced the center of the table with piping hot tea inside. They were asked to be seated, and delicate cookies were offered for the taking.

As tea was poured, Mrs. Jacobs asked, "Would you like one or two lumps of sugar?" Mike didn't know anything about tea, but sweet he knew he liked. "Two would be good," he replied. He watched the sugar dissolve. "This is cool!"

His awkward fingers barely fit through the fluted handle of the dainty cup that was offered. The two guests and Mrs. Jacobs talked about their weekends, a story the other student was writing, and about their families. That was always a hard subject for Mike. His mother had died earlier that year, and living in foster homes with two, sometimes three or four other strangers, was never easy.

The bell rang, the tea items were cleaned up, and everyone was forced to leave the retreat of the table for the next class. Mike knew this had been an out of the ordinary event, but he didn't really realize the full significance until much later. What he did know at this time was that the message had come through loud and clear. "I care about you. You are special."

Mike had somehow been able to overcome his rough childhood years. When he got out on his own, he used his natural math abilities and love for working with his hands and became the best mechanic at Joe's Automotive. He eventually started his own business and trained his own son in the trade. Maybe Mikey would follow in the same footsteps.

Attention was drawn back to his grandson. He seemed so young. Mike was thankful for the fact that his grandson's life was so much more stable than his own had been at the age of ten. God was like that. He could take that which was broken, and make it like new. Maybe that was what he liked so much about fixing cars. He could relate it so closely to what God had done in his life.

Again Mike's mind wandered. Though his memories spanned years of time, the thoughts ran through his head in a matter of seconds. This time, he recalled scanning the newspaper about ten years earlier. Something in the obituary column caught his attention. There was a familiar name, Julie Jacobs—he couldn't place it at first. Then he remembered. Of course, he never called his teacher by her first name. It was always Mrs. Jacobs. Skimming through the article, he read about her many years of devotion to her teaching career, her active life in her church, and the sons and grandchildren she was leaving behind.

The idea had come to him like a bolt of lightning. He wasn't sure at first how to make it happen, but with e-mail access, and the help of local media, the idea grew quickly. He knew she had offered tea to many of the students who had come through her room, and within no time at all the inspiration had grown.

At the memorial service there was an entire section of hundreds of teapots filled with flowers and notes from former students who had received not only the sharing of a cup of tea and crumpets, but the pouring out of love into their lives. As the minister presiding over the service shared the story of the teapots, he also explained in such simple terms the foundation of her love, Jesus Christ. Mike listened intently. He knew as his heart began to beat harder, that this was the kind of love he had been seeking for all of his life. There at the memorial service, he gave his life to the Lord.

Praying that simple prayer of forgiveness and acceptance of Jesus into his life was just the beginning. Mike and his wife had become involved in a great church and he was continuing to grow in his faith. Sometimes it pained him that it had taken him so long to find the answer for the emptiness he had often felt, yet pushed away. But now he was making up for lost time.

It seemed that all these church people wanted to do was go out for coffee. Mike had never been able to get into the coffee scene. Even when there was a Starbucks on every corner, he just couldn't quite acquire the taste for the bitter stuff. His cups of tea, on the other hand, would always be special.

It was time to get moving. Mikey was becoming antsy. Grandpa and grandson cleared the dishes from the table and prepared to go out on the lake. Mike sensed his responsibility clearly. Not only was he to continue brewing tea to pour into the teacups of important people in his life, but he was to pour out the love of Christ to all whom Christ loved. It gave him joy beyond words to watch how God could take the lumps of grief and pain in people's lives and dissolve them into a sweet peace that surpasses all understanding. Yes, life was good!

"And hope does not disappoint us, because God has poured out his love into our hearts by the Holy Spirit, whom he has given us."
Romans 5:5

Single-Cup Summary

- Christ died for us while we were still powerless sinners.
- Showing interest in someone and treating him/her as special helps break down emotional barriers.
- God can take what is broken and make it like new.
- We have a hunger in our hearts for God—an empty place in our souls that only God can fill.

 ## Grounded in the Word

- Romans 5:5-8
- Psalm 42:2
- 2 Corinthians 5:17

Points to Ponder and Percolate

ONLY GOD

Being confident of this, that he who began a good work in you will carry it on to completion until the day of Christ Jesus.
Philippians 1:6

There is a group of about twelve men who meet every Tuesday morning. They are salt of the Earth, and they meet at a coffee house that is one of the best on the Earth. Something divine happens just about every Tuesday. There is nothing in particular that bring these men together. They come from a variety of careers. There are those in construction, education, medicine, and social work. Their age groups span at least three generations. There are a few family ties, but for the most part they have very little in common.

The **common ground** for these men is their brokenness and the subsequent encouragement, accountability and spiritual strength they gain from their time together. They have all experienced pain or failure. There has been the pain of divorce, the pain of addiction, the pain of loss. There has been the failure to produce, the failure to provide, the failure to protect. They have found that over the past twenty years, it is not WHAT (scripture passage) they study, but THAT they study. Their commitment to meet together regularly has been the catalyst for their healing, as they dispense God's grace to each other.

As my husband and I met with Joe and his wife over a cup of coffee, Joe shared with us some of the miracles that have happened in these Tuesday morning men's lives. It is the accounting of what the Word, a cup of coffee, and doing life together can accomplish. It is a testament of the miracles that **only God** can perform.

Through the years, Joe has always had a heart for discipleship. From supporting his own three boys through their formative years, to working with church staff to develop a variety of discipleship programs, Joe has had many opportunities to hone his passion. God has given him the gifts of understanding and teaching. He has developed the wisdom that comes from the Word of God. It feels natural to him to share a passage of scripture and ask probing questions that get others talking and processing their own lives using the plumb line of God's Word.

About twenty years ago, one of the teens, now an adult, that Joe had mentored, came to him and asked if they could start a Bible study together. Scott had been through a painful divorce and was trying to raise his kids and make sense of life. His gift was hospitality, so they began meeting at Scott's house. He would fix an amazing breakfast of the "best French toast in the world," according to Joe. Then the men would meet in one of the other rooms of his home to fellowship and do some life together.

When Scott decided to sell his house, the group moved to the coffee shop. They continued to drill down underneath the surface of the scriptures and ask what it really meant to them and how it applied to their lives. Bill's life has been reshaped through this time together. His dysfunctional childhood family had left him angry— angry at the driver next to him, angry at work, angry with the church. He will be the first to tell you that he needed to bare and share his brokenness with this group. Over the years he has become a miracle of God's mercy and grace, a man being remade into Christ's likeness.

Mike was not a church attender at the time his little girl tragically drowned in their backyard pool. He fought depression and guilt, but he and his wife stuck together to move forward. Mike was touched by those who prayed for him, who didn't even know them. His eventual conversion was the catalyst for his family's healing. At some point during his recovery from his darkest days, God audibly spoke to him. He told him he would see his little girl again someday. God transformed his life into an amazing witness. He was dubbed the "metaphor man" because he could translate any life situation into a God moment. His relatable stories and willingness to be honest helps glue this group of men together.

Joe's dad joined them in 2007 after his wife of fifty-seven years lost her fight with cancer. Two of his boys came home from college and began working in the local school systems. They both came to the realization that they needed this fellowship. This family of strong believers had been through their own brokenness—death of a wife, infertility, a son diagnosed with autism. What better way to get through their pain than to fellowship with fellow believers.

Larry and his son, Limon, also attend the Tuesday mornings. Limon is living free of the grips of alcoholism. He is receiving courage and strength through these men, wise in their faith. Another one of Larry's sons, Todd, came to the group one day when he happened to be visiting from out of town. God's providence brought him there that day to hear a prayer request from one of the dads about his son's recent diagnosis of autism. Todd's field of expertise is working with individuals with special needs. He was able to share about the importance of early intervention, which started the anxious father on a path of research and help that has made all the difference with their son.

As Joe was sharing some of these stories, he brought up Philippians 1:6. He said that the guys anticipate this quote at least once a month. **"He who began a good work in you will carry it on to completion until the day of Christ Jesus"** (Philippians 1:6). As Joe states, "Every story can be rewritten." Steven has found relief from his loneliness. Andy has found purpose in his first trying year in education, and he and his wife have encompassed fulfillment in their adopted family. Travis has experienced comfort through his dad's healing from cancer. Al is finding renewed purpose in his late retirement years. Nothing that any of them goes through is a surprise to God, but **only God** can bring about the miracles. His answers sometimes come through His audible voice, and sometimes it comes though the voice of one of the men in the fellowship.

"It's interesting," says Joe. "The hub of the wheel has all these little spokes, but the hub is right there around a cup of coffee." Even some who don't join their circle find some benefits. They might sit off to the side, but can be seen leaning in to hear what the men are talking about. They are treated with respect and love. All are invited to join them. They sense something special about this group. When they are ready, they might become an additional spoke around the hub.

The Tuesday morning group occasionally breaks from fellowship to help work on a project. They have been known to take a collection for someone in need. They have been known to fund special ministries. They put their faith into action even when that faith requires digging into their pocketbooks.

Two years ago, Levi joined the group. He started out by joining them at a work project. His work ethic was amazing. He began to come on Tuesday mornings, and Joe was able to give him some part-time work. During his days at work with Joe, Joe helps him process the balancing of his family life, his work with the teens, leading of recovery groups, and working toward his pastor's license. This former drug addict is now addicted to Jesus. He is helping teens with parents who are drug addicts, and was lead to a thirteen-year-old living on the streets. He took him into his home, eventually gained guardianship over him, and is showing this Buddhist the way to the cross. When he walked into social services the case worker listened to the story and personally took on the job of making sure the paper work did not get lost in the shuffle. The Tuesday morning men's group were able to be a part of this miracle through both prayer and support.

A common theme as we wrapped up our conversation was from Hebrews 10:25. "**Let us not give up meeting together, as some are in the habit of doing, but let us encourage one another—and all the more as you see the Day approaching**." Christ is coming again! He wants us to gather together in love, commitment, caring, and sharing. We need each other. We can't worry too much about how or when we gather, but **THAT** we gather. God will use that time to continue His work in you! Commit to a fellowship and see what **only God** can do!

Single-Cup Summary

- Our common ground as humankind is that we either are broken, have been broken, or will be broken.
- Fellowship with other believers strengthens our bond through encouragement, accountability, and spiritual support.
- We should be intentional about meeting together to encourage one another.
- Every story can be rewritten.

 Grounded in the Word

- Philippians 1:6
- Hebrews 10:24-25
- Ezekiel 36:26-27

Points to Ponder and Percolate

UNCOMMONLY COMMON GROUND

Praise be to the God and Father of our Lord Jesus Christ, the Father of compassion and the God of all comfort, who comforts us in all our troubles, so that we can comfort those in any trouble with the comfort we ourselves have received from God. 2 *Corinthians 1:3-4*

We are lifted through life's journey amidst our sorrow and pain, our questions and confusions, through the compassion of one who has been through comparable situations. This can be seen over and over again. A family who is adopting is encouraged and mentored by another family who has already been through the process. The mom who is facing a prodigal child is comforted by another mom who has weathered similar circumstances. Someone who is fighting addiction receives support from a sponsor who has successfully broken through his or her own chains. Fresh grief is greeted with seasoned sorrow. Financial loss is met by those who have traded the importance of earthly goods for eternal treasure.

There is a Biblical explanation for this phenomenon. God allows His children to comfort each other with the same comfort that we have received from God. The solace usually finds its core in common pain. As you share your common personal encounters and sufferings with someone, you become amazed at the way your life's issues intersect. There are a few special people that cross your path with whom you find a particularly strong connection. God brings you together for His purpose.

My friend Shari developed a relationship like that in her work place. A teacher at the school where Shari worked began to open up to her. The more they talked, the more they were astonished at how similar their circumstances were. They discovered links in their lives which tightened the bonds of their relationship. First and foremost, they were both Christians, sharing the same faith and Spirit within their hearts. Katy's mom, who had also been a teacher, had a friend that was mutually loved and respected by both Katy and Shari. Katy's second son shared Shari's birthday.

As time progressed, their **common ground** began to center on their similar difficulties and heartbreak. Many times, they met over a cup of coffee as they shared the deep hurts of their past and current situations. Shari was a little further along on life's journey and had sensed the comfort of God through her troubles. Now it was her turn to encourage and comfort Katy, who was in the middle of the turmoil.

Their unfortunate common experience was that their first husbands had been unfaithful. They both had stories to tell. Shari, though now happily remarried, could relive her story through Katy's current circumstance. They shared the pain of feeling rejected multiple times, not being able to trust the one you loved, and trying to protect their dear little ones who were still at home.

Things came to a head one day when Katy found out that her husband had an illegitimate child through one of his affairs. Shari had been through the same situation with her first marriage, and she was able to relate once again to Katy's pain. Shari had been forced to draw boundaries, so she was able to help Katy get through her most painful days with both knowledge and hope. They worked through, cried through, and prayed through divorce, lack of child support, and the financial difficulties that were created from someone else's irresponsibility.

God was good through it all. Of course, He brought these two uncommonly common friends together. He also provided a workplace and a principal who was sensitive to the needs of his staff. On one particularly difficult day for Katy, the principal relieved her from her classroom and gave Shari permission to take her to coffee. He had watched their relationship transpire and he knew Shari would be able to help Katy through the tumult of that moment. For Katy, it was a comfort and relief to know that someone else had been through something similar, and that there was light at the end of the tunnel.

Darkness eventually turned to joy for Katy. She is happily remarried and moving forward in her family and her walk with God. Shari received some special blessings along the way as well. Katy's mom sent Shari a beautiful expression of her thanks. She had seen first-hand how this relationship had been a catalyst to seeing her daughter through her storm. When Shari retired, Katy set up a special luncheon with Shari and her friends to show her gratitude and love for this dear friend who had comforted her with the same comfort she had once found through God's compassion.

Recently, Shari saw that Katy had posted about some weight loss on Facebook. She was thrilled to be back into her skinny jeans. When she donned the once favorite pair of jeans, she found a note in her pocket. She took a picture of the note, an encouragement from Shari that had been hiding away as a precious treasure to be displayed on this day and time. It was a testament to the fact that she had experienced the compassion and comfort of the Heavenly Father through her dear sister in Christ.

No one is exempt from pain in life. It might be through tragedy, loss, poor choices, or someone else's poor choices. There is someone who has been down a similar path who can help you. You may be the one to help someone else who is going through the tough journey you once faced. Let the praise go to the God and Father of our Lord Jesus Christ, who designed you to count on Him to help you face your problems and then uses your specific circumstances to comfort others. You are right where God needs you to be. He may have someone about to enter your path who has been through almost exactly what you have been through. His timing and placement is amazing and perfectly orchestrated to bring about His sweet will for your life.

Sometimes it's tough to relive your troubles. The victory comes in the fact that not only can you comfort someone else, but your own burden lifts a little in the process. The perspective of your time-tested scars reminds you of God's goodness and His healing of your wounds.

Single-Cup Summary

- We are lifted through life's journey amidst our sorrow and pain, our questions and confusions, through the compassion of one who has been through comparable situations.
- God provides special people to help give you comfort.
- Even in the midst of your trials you can see God's goodness as you take refuge in Him.
- Though it may be painful to look back on your trials, remembering how the hand of God helped you brings healing and allows you to help someone else.

 ## Grounded in the Word

- 2 Corinthians 1:3-4
- Romans 8:28
- Psalm 34:8
- Hebrews 12:11

Points to Ponder and Percolate

IT'S FREE!

It is for freedom that Christ has set us free. Stand firm, then, and do not let yourselves be burdened again by a yoke of slavery.
Galatians 5:1

A long time ago, in a galaxy far, far away, I was in college. I suppose I may be exaggerating a little, but I did just have my fortieth year reunion last fall. My coffee habit was not yet established back then. I drank coffee primarily when I needed a boost of energy for studying. I can partially blame my husband for getting me started. While we were still dating, we would occasionally pull all-nighters studying for finals. To keep us awake, we would take our text books and binders full of notes to a nearby twenty-four-hour coffee shop. We would get a cup of coffee and an English muffin, and study the night away.

The restaurant that we frequented for this activity is now called the Point Loma Café. It has changed hands a few times, but in the 1970's this particular restaurant gave out free coffee chips. You would receive one as you paid for your meal, and you could use it at your next visit. Being the frugal college students that we were, we took advantage of this offer. I'm not sure how many refills we would get while sitting there with our noses in the books, but I know we got the better end of that deal!

It would be ridiculous to conjecture that after we received our "free" coffee, we would ask the manager if we could wash the dishes or sweep the floors to pay for it. You can't pay for something that is free! I'm sure we would have been patted on the back and told not to burden ourselves with trying to work for the goods we had received. Back in the dish room, the staff would probably be throwing their hands up in confusion as they discussed those foolish college kids.

As easy as it is for us to see the futility in trying to pay for our free coffee, we are sometimes blinded to the fact that we do that very thing in our walk with Christ. He wants us to be free, and has already paid the price for our freedom. We foolishly try to "buy" it, burdening ourselves with a yoke of slavery, by working hard, serving well, or adhering strongly to the law. I wonder if Jesus goes into the throne room and throws up His hands saying, "When will they learn that their attempt to be justified by the law has no value. The only thing that counts is faith expressing itself through love" (see Galatians 5:6).

In *More Coffee Shop Theology,* by Frank Moore, he states that many people think that God places all our good deeds on one side of His balance scales and our bad deeds on the other side. If the good outweighs the bad, we receive entrance into the Streets of Gold. God's Word clearly lets us know that our acts of righteousness are like filthy rags when it comes to gaining His favor (see Isaiah 64:6). Try purchasing something at the store with a bag of dirty, oily rags. It won't get you very far! It is because of Christ's sacrifice on the cross, not our good performance, that the Father sees us through eyes of grace and mercy. We are declared free from the guilt and penalty of our past sins. Since God no longer condemns those who are in Christ Jesus (see Romans 8:1), we should not condemn ourselves or be slaves to the guilt of our pasts.[3]

Today, as I write this, it is Good Friday. On this special day, we ponder and worship the Christ who suffered on the cross for us. This was an amazing act of love planned for the human race, that we might receive atonement for our sins once and for all. All we need to do is accept His payment for our sins through faith. When we realize and experience the freedom that comes through forgiveness and a reconciled relationship with God the Father, our natural outpouring should be expressed in love for God and for each other.

Serving one another in love and loving your neighbor as yourself is now done with a whole new perspective. You are not earning your way to Heaven based on how many meals you serve to the homeless or how often you give to the poor. You are not a better person if you volunteer for as many jobs as you can handle at your church. You are not getting a ticket in to the Pearly Gates because you are a great rule follower. Your motive is not to receive accolades from God or man. Your life and service overflow as an expression of gratefulness for God's gift to you.

When you smile and say a kind word to the harried mom surrounded by misbehaving kids, it is because God has smiled down on you. You want to extend a little of who He is to someone else. As you serve the homeless, you can pray for them and value them because God saw value in you. You deal daily with your sinful nature because you want to live for Christ, not for yourself. Being less selfish or more patient will not buy your way into God's grace.

---

[3] Moore, Frank. *More Coffee Shop Theology, Translating Doctrinal Jargon Into Everyday Life*. Kansas City: Beacon Hill Press, 1998.

You already have His love and grace, His peace and joy. These gifts just make you want to be more like Him, and you want others to see Christ in you.

God's grace is sufficient, and it doesn't cost you anything. Open your heart, and let His love and forgiveness overflow in your life. It's liberating! And it's FREE!

 ## Single-Cup Summary

- We can't pay for something that is free.
- Christ has already paid the price for our freedom.
- Our good deeds are like filthy rags before our Holy God.
- It is because of Christ's death on the cross that God sees us through His grace and mercy.
- All we need to do is accept His payment for our sins through faith.
- God's grace is sufficient!

 ## Grounded in the Word

- Galatians 5:1-6
- Isaiah 64:6
- Romans 8:1
- Ephesians 2:8-9
- 2 Corinthians 12:9

 *Points to Ponder and Percolate*

A DRINK OFFERING

But even if I am being poured out like a drink offering on the sacrifice and service coming from your faith, I am glad and rejoice with all of you. Philippians 2:17

In the Old Testament, the Israelites were directed to present offerings to God. When more than one offering was bestowed, there was usually a specific procedure. First they would provide a sin or guilt offering. Next they would give an offering of consecration and complete surrender to God. Finally, they would offer a fellowship offering as a voluntary act of worship, thanksgiving and fellowship. It included a communal meal. Part of this communion was the drink offering, which usually amounted to a little more than a quart of wine that was poured around the base of the altar. This sequence signified: 1) that sin was dealt with; 2) the worshiper committed himself completely to God; 3) fellowship or communion between the Lord and the worshiper was established.

We no longer have to bring offerings like this to God because Jesus' death and resurrection offered a once-for-all sacrifice. Yet God still expects us to deal with our sin, commit ourselves to Him, and have fellowship with Him. New Testament Christians are exhorted to offer our bodies as living sacrifices, holy and pleasing to God (see Romans 12:1). Rather than being caught up in ritual, we are to involve our heart, mind, and will in allowing God to transform us into what we are called to be: dead to sin and alive to

God. God loves this kind of true worship. He especially enjoys our praise and thanksgiving.

In the Philippians 2:17 passage, Paul was feeling a little at the end of his rope, being in prison for possibly the last time before a martyr's death. He had given his life and teachings to so many, and now he was able to rejoice with those whom he had served and who were continuing to work out their faith. His life and his ministry were an offering of thanksgiving, flowing into those he loved. Like Paul, we have so much to be grateful for, but sometimes we feel weary from serving. As we pour out our lives for others, a cup of coffee can be the perfect pit stop to offer thanksgiving. The break may be just what you need, and it gives you a chance to stretch your legs and say a prayer.

I was recently at the home of my youngest son and family. The occasion was the birth of their second child, a precious little boy. My job was to serve them in any way they needed as their family adjusted to this long anticipated change in their lives. I cooked some meals, did some shopping, walked the dog, and cared for their four-year-old, so that they could figure out some semblance of a routine with their newborn. Having become accustomed to my recent retired life, this was all a little bit exhausting. It was, however, worth every second. My morning coffee was a sweet time to reflect on the blessings and joys of this event.

One afternoon my son and I took a long walk, got an afternoon pick-me-up at a local caffeine station, and did some of the grocery shopping together. Our conversation became deep as we discussed our broken world and the many confusing and frustrating dichotomies of our culture. Though we didn't agree on everything, we were unified in our belief that God is in control. He is the one with the answers to the mysteries of life. His Word is true and relevant more so now than ever, and we need to continue to seek Him and grow in grace and truth. I sensed that we both came away from our discussion as better people, learning to listen to and love each other more deeply.

Our time together over a walk and a cup of coffee became a type of drink offering. We shared about how his time as a young boy in our home and in our church, good and bad alike, helped shape him into who he is today. I reminisced about how we cherished our times when the boys were growing up from infancy through young adulthood. My son and his wife are similarly cherishing their time with their daughter and their new son. As parents, our greatest prayer and desire for our children is not that they think and act just like us, but that they love, serve, and imitate Christ. I am forever glad and rejoice over their faith. It makes any and all sacrifices during their childhood very worthwhile!

My first few days there were also shared with the other grandma, called Coco. We made a pretty good pair as we tag-teamed some of the chores and snuggling with our new grandson. We had a great time, as well, sharing and praising God for his goodness. One morning, Coco told me about one of her dear life-long friends, Rita, who had poured out her life for her family. Instead of celebrating new life, Rita was cherishing the end days with her mother.

Rita's mom lived about an hour away. During the last couple years of her mom's life, Rita would drive the sixty-minute distance after a long week at work to minister to her mom's needs. She was an angel to this woman who had lived a life of faithfulness to her Savior. Now in her final days, she was receiving back a small portion of what she had often bestowed on others. In this unique role reversal, Rita would fix her mom something to eat, attend to her needs, and tuck her into bed at night. Though this routine was physically and emotionally draining, Rita was thankful for the opportunity to love on her mom.

Her drive to and from her mom's home became a time of worship, as Rita would pray and sing praise songs. She had her regular drink stop for a Tuxedo Mocha, a little white chocolate and a little dark chocolate mixed into her coffee. She often expressed guilt about the calories of this frequented treat, but it also helped to fuel her. She would stop, get her coffee, stretch her legs, walk a bit, and pray, before getting back into the car. She remembers using a coffee stop to write her mom's obituary and reflect on treasured moments in her life. She used the liquid refreshment as a drink offering being poured out on the service coming from her faith.

Now that her mom is gone, Rita continues to make a weekend coffee run. She uses this time to treat herself, have a quiet time, and to think and pray intentionally for others. She calls it her "sip and prayer" time. Interestingly enough, one of her favorite spots is called **Common Ground**s Coffee. She often will pick up a friend for coffee to hopefully bring a little light to someone else's life. Her weekend routine is not as grueling these days, but it is still used as a time to fellowship and commune with the Lord.

Coffee, tea, or soda breaks do not necessarily have to be shared with another person. They can be enjoyed alone as an opportunity to offer thanksgiving for those whom God has placed in our lives. Use your time to thank God for those who have served you. Thank Him for those you are currently serving. Are your efforts wearing at times? Of course! That's why they are called sacrifices, but they are worth the cost! Grab a drink and present yourself as a drink offering of thanksgiving and praise to God!

 ## Single-Cup Summary

- We are to offer ourselves as living sacrifices, holy and pleasing to God.
- God loves the true worship of His people, and it is good to praise the Lord.
- Sometimes we feel weary from serving, but we continue to pour ourselves out like a drink offering of thanks.
- We can use our coffee treats or other "pit stops" to pray, thank God for His presence in our lives, and commune with Him.

 ## Grounded in the Word

- Philippians 2:17
- Romans 12:1
- John 4:24
- Psalm 92:1-2
- Galatians 6:9

 *Points to Ponder and Percolate*

OPEN THE DOOR!

Here I am! I stand at the door and knock. If anyone hears my voice and opens the door, I will come in and eat with him, and he with me. Revelation 3:20

One of my favorite sounds is the excited voices of my grandkids at my front door. When they arrive at our house, they ring the doorbell over and over to announce their presence. They can't wait to come in, but they stand there (or wiggle and jump) in anticipation for the door to be opened. As soon as they are invited in, the party begins! There are hugs and laughter all round. They compete for our attention, each one trying to speak over their sibling to tell us the latest and greatest things that have happened to them at school or at home. We wouldn't think of leaving them out on the front porch ringing, knocking, and begging to come inside.

Jesus is just as excited to visit with us. He stands at our heart's door and knocks. He calls to us, hoping we will hear His voice. His desire is that we would allow Him in so that we can build relationship together. The fellowship and shared meals with Him are more than we could ever imagine. The problem is that we don't always recognize His voice and His knock, at least not at first. There is this longing in our spirit for something more. We desire to be closer to God, we just don't know how to draw near to Him. We aren't even aware that all of these longings are His way of drawing us closer to opening the door to a new life with Him.

God's pursuit of us was brought to life during the Easter Sunday service at Olive Knolls Nazarene Church in 2018. Senior Pastor Darren's message centered on Jesus bringing us resurrected hope. The central text came from Luke 24 when two men met Jesus on the Road to Emmaus. They didn't recognize Jesus at first. They were blinded by their own hopelessness. Jesus walked with them for miles explaining all that was said in the Scriptures concerning Himself. At the end of their journey, they invited Him to stay with them. As Jesus broke bread with them, they suddenly recognized who He was. After He left them, they reflected on their resurrected Savior and their new found hope. "They asked each other, 'Were not our hearts burning within us while He talked with us on the road and opened the Scriptures to us?'" (Luke 24:32).

My friend, Kelly, felt a similar burning call in her spirit to a life of hope, peace, and refreshment. She didn't exactly understand at the time that the God of Hope was the One pursuing her. She was thirsty for the water that can only be offered by the Wellspring of Life, and she was hungry for the rich fare that can only be offered by the Bread of Life. She had grown up believing in God, and she knew she wanted to feel His presence in her life. She was sensing a knocking at her heart's door. She just didn't know how to begin opening herself up to this type of intimate relationship with the Lord. Since she had been raised in the Catholic faith, she felt like it was important to get her own children into church. She visited some churches, but nothing seemed to fit. Her kids complained and were miserable.

Around this time, Kelly met Jen. Their boys were in the same class in school, and they shared the same Boy Scout Troop. The two moms divided duties in the boys' classroom as well as at the Scout meetings. Kelly was drawn to Jen. Though their friendship started based on these surface encounters, they seemed to have a lot of **common ground**. They enjoyed working together, and their relationship began to grow slowly.

During this time, Jen experienced a tragic loss. Kelly was struck by the gravity of the situation. Even though she didn't know the details at the time, Kelly was moved to help Jen. Kelly said that she was able to put a bandage over her own secret pain by helping someone else who was hurting. With her gift of hospitality, she got the Scouts involved in taking meals and raising money. She helped care for Jen's boys, picked up groceries, and eventually invited Jen to lunch at The Country Rose Tea Garden, where she worked part-time.

They sat over tea and scones and salad for about three hours. They learned more about each other, shared deeply, and cried together. They spoke of God, and Kelly was amazed at the depth of Jen's faith. Kelly felt so connected to Jen, and knew she needed to stay linked to her. Their friendship deepened from this point, and a few weeks later, Jen invited Kelly to her church, Olive Knolls Nazarene Church.

Kelly accepted the invitation. She remembers exactly what she wore: cute jeans, a white shirt with a necklace, and some black boots. Kelly told me that she bawled through the worship songs. She cried through the sermon. She could not get it together. She took communion and one of the serving pastors, Pastor Theron, prayed with her. She knew this was home. They would not go anywhere else. God met her there. Not only that, but when she picked up the kids from Sunday school, they were so excited. They had loved it, and on the way home they chattered about the things they had done and sang the songs they had learned.

From that point, Kelly and Jen began walking together. They would talk, and Jen would teach Kelly about God and what His Word meant. Though Kelly had learned the basics growing up, she didn't really understand the treasures that were there for her. She had always known that God was watching over her and that she could pray to Him, but now she was learning that there was so much more to knowing Jesus! She had been searching for this greater intimacy without even realizing it.

Through the divine intervention of this special friendship, God saved Kelly from her anxiety and her fear. God had known all along how shattered she was. He knew that Jen was going to be the vehicle to draw Kelly closer to God. As they shared in brokenness together, God broke through. Kelly realized that it was Jesus that had been knocking at her heart. Once she opened the door and let Him fully in, she found healing and restoration. The blinders fell off, and Scripture came alive! She learned that Satan had been feeding her lies about herself, and her new life in Christ was providing healthy coping skills that brought her out of a life of being chained to defeat.

Over and over again in God's Word we receive invitations from Jesus. He says, "Come to me all you who are weary and burdened, and I will give you rest" (Matthew 11:28). He invites, "Come, all you who are thirsty" (Isaiah 55:1). He waits patiently for us as He knocks at our door, so that He may come in and have fellowship and communion with us. Are you weary, thirsty, hungry, or hopeless? Don't leave Him out on the front porch! Listen to His voice! Open the Door!

Single-Cup Summary

- Jesus stands at our heart's door and knocks.
- We don't always recognize His voice at first, but He is waiting to fill the longing in our spirit for something more.
- When we open ourselves to Christ, our blinders fall off and we recognize that Satan has been feeding us lies.
- Jesus invites us over and over to come to Him.

 ## Grounded in the Word

- Revelation 3:20
- Luke 24:13-35
- Matthew 11:28-30
- Isaiah 55:1

Points to Ponder and Percolate

A HEARTBEAT FOR GOD

My flesh and my heart may fail, but God is the strength of my heart and my portion forever. Psalm 73:26

Joyce found me after church! "I don't drink coffee, but I have a story for you!" She quickly explained that because of her heart condition, she had to give up tea and soda. Though she liked the smell of coffee, she had never acquired a taste for it. Pure water was her drink of choice, so we sipped some together as we shared **common ground** on my patio. It was a beautiful spring day, a rare occurrence in Bakersfield. Her story began to unfold.

Joyce and Al's son, AJ, fought a three year battle with lung cancer. During that time, Joyce got really good at being "Mama Bear," in order to stand up for her boy. Because he had a terminal illness, the hospital would often give him less than stellar treatment for some of his residual effects. They would want to write a prescription or send him away without even seeing the doctor. Joyce would take control and get the service he needed.

At 26 years of age, AJ had been given three months to live. He lived three **years!** He lived well to the end. He told his mom that if he had not had cancer, he very well might have spent eternity in Hell. Instead, this dreaded disease drew him closer to God, and he lived his last years praising God and witnessing to others of His goodness. "Mama Bear," however, had to grapple with her need to control her circumstances.

Joyce admitted that she was angry that God did not heal AJ. During a Bible study in Acts, she had a moment of revelation. When Peter and John passed by the temple gate and saw the crippled man, God's name was glorified through his healing. It dawned on her as she studied this passage that Jesus had walked by that gate numerous times during His ministry on Earth, but He had chosen not to heal this man at those times. It gave her comfort to realize that God has a purpose and perfect timing in all that He does or does not do. She stopped being so angry, and began to be grateful for the three extra years that she had to spend with their son.

Though this helped her to begin to deal with her grief in a more healthy way, she still had issues with control. The need to manipulate her situations would cause her to be anxious, to the point of having to take valium in order to just make it through a dentist appointment. She handled her problems with anger, frustration, and self-imposed power.

In December of 2016, Joyce and Al changed insurance. Joyce made sure before she switched that she would be able to keep her primary doctor, maintain her cardiologist, and continue to use San Joaquin Hospital. Her aversion to Memorial Hospital had nothing to do with the quality of the hospital. It came from the memories that would flood, due to the fact that AJ had been taken there for his treatments. Everything checked out, so they switched over. When the New Year rolled around, however, the insurance contracts suddenly changed. Neither her cardiologist nor San Joaquin Hospital was any longer on the approved list. She was losing her grip on the ability to manage her life!

The new cardiologist wanted to do a complete work-up on her heart. Joyce has a strong heart that pumps great. It just has problems with the electrical impulses traveling in a consistent path. Certain triggers cause it to go into atrial fibrillation (AFib). The tests showed a 90% blockage, and Joyce needed to go in immediately for an angiogram and to have stints put in. At the same time an ultrasound of her thyroid showed nodules, so she needed to have a biopsy done. She had to be off blood thinners for the biopsy, but on the blood thinners for the angiogram. She had to have the biopsy before the angiogram, but there wasn't an opening for the procedure for three weeks.

Joyce was beside herself. She was responding to people with screaming and anger. She was supposed to go to Memorial hospital, with a doctor she had never met. Her Bible study leader, Donna, prayed with her. Joyce knew she needed to give her physical heart as well as her emotional and mental attitudes to God. So she prayed, "Lord, I give it all to you, just fix it so I can go to San Joaquin (hospital)." God said, "No, you are going to have to give it **all** to me." So she tried her prayer again, "Ok, God, it's yours! Period!" Soon thereafter, an opening was made available for her biopsy. With that completed, she was able to make her angiogram appointment.

She decided to sing praises on her way to the pre-op meeting, but when she walked into the front door of Memorial hospital, she started bawling. The pre-op nurse immediately came to her assistance and asked if she was nervous about the procedure. Joyce shared the source of her difficulties of coming to this particular hospital and the recollections of AJ's cancer that flooded her each time she entered. The nurse said, "Let me pray with you."

She even offered to let her come through a different entrance the next day, so that Joyce wouldn't have to be faced with some of the memories.

The bonding with this nurse wasn't Joyce's plan. It was God's plan. By letting go, she received her first of many amazing blessings during this experience. The next day, Joyce confidently went through the front doors with peace. As she was wheeled into the pre-op area, she passed the room where one of AJ's surgeries had occurred. She cried, but the tears were not tears of panic. They were just sad tears.

In pre-op, two nurses were attending to her. This was unusual. Joyce soon realized that God was again blessing her. One nurse was setting up her IV's and prep for surgery. The other was holding her hand and talking to her. She was a specialist in grief counseling. The pre-op nurse had written some of the issues on Joyce's chart. The grief counselor had even taken the time to look up AJ's surgery and was not afraid to talk to Joyce about his life and his death. Joyce was able to turn this into a time to remember the positive things about AJ.

Then, the doctor came in. His conversation with Joyce was very reassuring. He felt they could do the angiogram by going through her wrist, which would be much less intrusive than what had previously been planned. He asked questions and listened to Joyce's concerns. He made the procedure as patient-friendly as possible. The anesthesiologist talked with her through the procedure and helped alleviate her fears and discomfort throughout the surgery. Shortly after Joyce went to post-op she was sitting up, eating a turkey sandwich, and dismissed within two hours. The results showed no obstruction anywhere!

As Joyce began to thank God for healing her heart, Satan whispered his deceit into her mind. He questioned her why God would heal her heart and let her son die. Joyce grappled with this question a couple of days before telling Satan to get behind her. God touched her, and she knew it! He healed her physical heart, and He gave her spiritual heart peace and joy!

When your heart beats for God, he strengthens you and gives you exactly what you need. When you stop trying to be in control of your life, God is able to work in His way and His time. He knows what you need so much better than you do. What areas in your life do you need to let go? Holding tightly to them is like placing a vice on your own heart. Let go, and let God bless you and be your portion.

 Single-Cup Summary

- Many times we fight God for control of our circumstances.
- When we lose our grip on managing our lives, we can become anxious, angry, and frustrated.
- When we give everything to God, holding nothing back, He brings us peace and His blessings.
- Waiting on God and His timing and purpose is always perfect.
- As we submit to God and draw near to Him, we can resist the devil, and the devil will flee from us.

Grounded in the Word

- Psalm 73:26
- Philippians 4:6–7
- Psalm 27:14
- Acts 3:1–10
- James 4:7–8

Points to Ponder and Percolate

_____

_____

_____

_____

_____

_____

_____

_____

_____

_____

_____

_____

_____

_____

_____

_____

_____

_____

_____

_____

_____

CIRCLE THE WAGONS

Whether you turn to the right or to the left, your ears will hear a voice behind you saying, "This is the way; walk in it." Isaiah 30:21

I met Linda about three years ago. We had a women's ministry at Olive Knolls Nazarene Church called LIFT (Ladies in Fellowship Together). We met together once a month on Monday evenings. We shared a potluck of goodies, tea or coffee, and an evening of worship, fellowship, and teaching. Since I led worship, I was thrilled to hear that Linda loved to sing. When I heard her voice, I was even more excited! She harmonized beautifully, and she was soon a part of our team.

On each of these Monday nights, different women from our church took turns sharing their story or leading us in a Bible study. We would then answer questions together around circular tables of six to eight ladies. This format helped us to get to know each other a little better, but we always made it clear that no one would be forced to share if they weren't comfortable. As a ministry team we recognized the deep need for women to know they were not doing life alone. We wanted to be open and vulnerable, but we also knew that everyone needed to go at their own pace. We wanted this to be a safe place, a circle of protection.

During the nineteenth century, pioneers who traveled in large wagon trains across the country worked together to reach their destination. The power in numbers helped them assist each other, navigate the rough terrain, and make sure they were keeping on course. If they were under attack or vulnerable to an enemy, they would place their schooners together in a circle to provide a protective barrier and cover of defense.

The "circle the wagons" idiom today means to prepare to defend against attack or criticism. Our attacks come from the judgements and criticisms of others, our own self-condemning thoughts, and from the father of lies, Satan, himself. We need groups of Christians, fellow travelers along this rough terrain of life, to help support and defend us. This happens through prayer, leading each other to God's truths and promises, and sharing how our own brokenness and pain has ended in triumph.

It was in this context that Linda learned to let go of the idea of trying to appear perfect. Through the compassion and wisdom of other women she began to open herself up to who God was calling her to be. At a recent women's retreat, Linda shared her story. She was gracious enough to let me include it in *Common Ground.*

As a child and teen Linda grew up in a strong Christian home. She had a strong faith, was never tempted to party or cuss, and believed that her relationship with Christ set her apart. She attended a Christian university, and she continued to sing, wear a smile, and partner with God to save the world. She was known for her fun personality and happy disposition.

When Linda got married, it became increasingly impossible to live up to her self-imposed image. In fact, she says, "It was exhausting!" Reality hit. She could not keep up that image every day, all day. She was also facing a perfect storm. She moved back to Bakersfield after 10 years, and she found herself with no friends, a new job, and an unknown illness that affected her daily. For the first time in her life, she didn't like who she was. She saw herself as selfish, fake, and judgmental.

During this time, she met someone who only saw the confident, funny, carefree parts of her that she chose to show. "This was the 'me' that I was most comfortable with; the role I had played for so long, the Linda I wanted to be," Linda explained. After a short time of unfaithfulness, she confessed to her husband, and they were separated for a period.

Because of her apparent failures and self-incrimination, Linda avoided church for seventeen years. She didn't want people to ask her, "How are you?" She didn't want people to know her—to know that she was human and not set apart. She pretty much alienated herself from people until she was invited to a Bunco group by her best friend. This seemed like a safe place to get to know a few people. It was a huge step in letting people in. Conversation didn't get too serious, and most of the time she could just laugh and let go.

Bunco gave Linda some confidence to try a monthly Bible study called LIFT. She loved the singing and listening to the speaker, but would feel a physical wall going up when the small groups shared around the table. Throughout those Monday nights she would hear about others' pain, petitions, and triumphs. It opened her eyes to the fact that everyone has a story. She was sitting at tables with broken people, like herself, in need of a Savior. She heard ladies speak about God's grace, and decided it wasn't for her. She heard others speak of God's will for our lives, which she felt she had already squandered due to marital unfaithfulness. When someone said, "God wants the best for you," Linda wanted to correct their tense. She was more comfortable with, "God wantED the best for me."

One evening, Linda finally could not hold it in any longer. She started crying. I remember that night well. My new friend was finally letting God and us in, just a little. She explained that she had made some choices in her life that put her on a different path than the one God originally intended, a path that was "less than." She shared that her path was full of consequences and penance. One of the ladies shared that God had another path for her. She was encouraged by the verse, "Whether you turn to the right or to the left, you will hear a voice behind you saying, 'This is the way; walk in it" (Isaiah 30:23). We were all crying and began to lift her up in prayer. Though she didn't like the attention at the time, she can look back now and feels so grateful.

Over time Linda has learned to stop punishing herself and accepting the lie that she is doomed to an inferior life. She has learned that she doesn't have to continue to nail herself to the cross for being human. She said, "Christ did that for me. Even when I left Him, He never left me. He relentlessly pursued me."

The Bible study gave Linda the boost she needed to attend her first women's retreat. The topic of the weekend was "Perfectly Imperfect." She knew this was exactly where God wanted her to be. As she learned about how God wants to use us, flawed and all, redeemed for His purpose, she finally broke down. One of her sweet Bunco friends prayed with her. She began a road to healing and purpose.

Three years later, Linda has been faithfully attending church. She has kept herself surrounded with a team of women who continue to pray for her, show compassion, and share wisdom. She has become intentional about spending time with other Christian women. Linda became brave and vulnerable enough to share her story with two hundred women at the following year's retreat. Now her story is helping others as they relate to her new self: broken, but forgiven.

God is continuing to work! Linda is now a leader in women's ministries. She strongly believes in the importance of "circling the wagons" for each other. I encourage each of you to pray about who needs the protection and defense of your prayers and support. Then take action! Obey that still small voice! If you are, like Linda, one who is afraid to let your walls down, who feels like you need to hide yourself behind a smile or false image, let God begin to break down the barriers. Reach out to someone at your local church or Bible study. God is ready to forgive and heal your wounds, no matter how deep!

 ## Single-Cup Summary

- Our attacks come from the judgements and criticism of others, our own self-condemning thoughts, and from the father of lies, Satan, himself.
- We need fellow travelers along the rough terrain of life to help circle and defend us through prayer, God's Word, and sharing together.
- God has a path for all of us that brings restoration, forgiveness, and healing.

Grounded in the Word

- Isaiah 30:21
- 1 John 3:19-20
- John 8:44
- Philippians 2:1-4
- Psalm 103:1-13

Points to Ponder and Percolate

IMITATING FAITH

Remember your leaders, who spoke the word of God to you.
Consider the outcome of their way and imitate their faith.
Hebrews 13:7

It was mid-April, and I had been invited to a women's ministry tea at a neighboring church. I knew I was underdressed when I stepped out of my car and mothers and daughters, friends and family, were decked to the hilt in their spring best and donned in beautiful hats. This was a BIG deal. The tables were festively decorated in pastel colors, flowers, and striking table favors. The planners and table hosts had thought of everything! This was more than **common ground!** We had been invited to share extraordinary ground!

By the way, it didn't matter that I wasn't dressed to the "tea." (I couldn't resist the pun.) Just as God loves us and receives us just as we are, I was accepted and drawn into this lovely event just as I was, in my capris and sandals. As the program started, we were treated to great worship music. The food was superb, the door prizes fantastic, and the games and activities fun and engaging. I was surrounded by a few of my long-time friends and a few new ones. What a privilege to be a part of this occasion!

The speaker shared about our responsibility as women to mentor others. She sited multiple examples in the Bible. Jesus discipled and mentored the Twelve. Paul encouraged and taught Barnabus.

Elizabeth listened to and counseled Mary. We were reminded of those who had spoken into our lives, and we were inspired to be intentional about finding others to guide.

At the end, the Master of Ceremonies, Lynn, affirmed that she had women in her life that had mentored her. She was continuing to look to other godly women for counsel and strength, teaching, and wisdom. She mentioned a few people by name, and included my friend, Patti, who was sitting to my left. Patti had actually been her MOPS (Mother of Pre Schoolers) Mentor Mom. This young woman, now in charge of this grand party, had been a new Christian at the time. She was receptive to Patti's sweet guidance and counsel, and now Lynn was teaching her daughters and other young women. Patti was surprised and honored to be pointed out. She remembered talking to Lynn over a cup of coffee and nurturing her faith. I looked at Patti and whispered, "I need to write down your story!"

Patti and I met a few weeks later. She started off by reminiscing about a program called "Heart to Heart." In this program, a mentor woman was paired with a younger woman in our church. Patti was fairly new to the church and had recently recommitted her life to God. She was paired with the leader, Marsha Chamberlain. They developed a relationship that is strong to this day, and the modeling that she received was a catalyst to Patti developing a heart for helping other women.

Patti explained that a MOPS Mentor Mom's job was to come along side younger moms, encourage them, be a sounding board, and give them guidance. Many of the MOPS moms were unchurched, so it was also an opportunity to share Jesus with them. They would meet twice a month for fellowship and a speaker. Patti said that it didn't matter who was there on a given day, God always showed up. One of the women Patti remembered was having some struggles with her marriage. Not only was Patti able to advise her, but she and her husband, Eldon, met with the couple together. Eldon was able to speak truth into the young husband.

Being able to meet with people in a more casual setting, over coffee or a meal, enabled women to open up a little more. It was an avenue to breathe life and love into someone else, and show them how to live out their walk with God. The relationships that were built eventually opened other doors. Patti and Eldon were later able to lead a small young couple's group. The couples looked up to them and gleaned healthy marriage practices. They were able to talk about the ups and downs all marriages go through. They were able to communicate about the work, commitment, and perseverance it takes to make a good marriage great.

Patti shared how it was fun to watch the girls under her grow in their roles as moms and wives. She had shared with them during one of the sessions that their family had a Thanksgiving tablecloth. Whoever shared the Thanksgiving meal with them would sign and date the table-cloth. Recently Patti was tagged in a Facebook post. It was from a young mom from her MOPS group who was sharing about the tablecloth tradition that their family had begun, giving credit to and thanking Patti for the idea.

Patti mentioned that you don't always know if you have had an influence on someone. Your lives may part or move on in different directions for a season. You may never know what type of impact you have had. Then, every once in a while, you are blessed by being somewhere when someone thanks you for what your efforts meant to them.

As we concluded our lunch together, we had come full circle. Patti once again remembered the huge impact Marsha had in her life. Because someone else had taken the time to speak the Word of God to her, Patti had been able to imitate and continue the cycle of mentoring that had been shown to her.

What a lesson we can take from this! If you are a young Christian, reach out to a more seasoned Christian who can coach you, listen to your questions and concerns, and help you to grow in your faith. If someone has done this for you in the past, take a minute to think about others around you. Be intentional about who might need a word of encouragement or a chance to share their hurts or needs. Remember those who did this for you, and imitate their faith!

 ## Single-Cup Summary

- We have the unique privilege and responsibility to mentor those who are young in the faith.
- The Bible has many examples of mentoring relationships.
- Sometimes we are blessed to find out that we have made an impact on someone's walk with Christ.
- When someone takes the time to speak into our life, we are than able to imitate or continue the cycle of mentoring.
- Be intentional about building relationships to encourage others in their faith.

Grounded in the Word

- Hebrews 13:7
- Matthew 5:1-12
- Acts 13:1-3
- Luke 1:39-44

Points to Ponder and Percolate

HARD PRESSED

We are hard pressed on every side, but not crushed; perplexed, but not in despair; persecuted, but not abandoned; struck down, but not destroyed. 2 Corinthians 4:8-9

There is a common thread, **common ground**, if you will, between things that are pressed. When you press flowers between pages of a book, it may seem as if the plant is being destroyed. The final result, however, is to preserve the beautiful blooms as well as the memories associated with them. Apples must be pressed beyond recognition between the planks of the cider mill to coax the sweet juice from the applied force. Wrinkled clothing gets pressed by a hot iron. The result is a smooth garment ready for presentation in public. Only through years of the pressing of particles of mud, sand, and remains of plants and animals, is sedimentary rock formed. What seems to be pressure beyond reason is actually part of the process of making something better.

Being "hard pressed" implies struggle. It is associated with the poor or impoverished. No one really wants to be "hard pressed on every side," but it is almost a certainty that we will face a time in our lives when we feel like we are about to be crushed. God knew humans would be vulnerable. After all, we are just jars of clay (see 2 Corinthians 4:7). That's why He sent Jesus to let His light shine out of darkness (see 2 Corinthians 4:6). He exchanges death for life, alienation for love, condemnation for mercy and grace.

To illustrate this idea, I began thinking about my latest Mother's Day gift. This year I got a French Press. I can't tell you how happy this made me! We were getting ready for a rather lengthy road trip, and I wanted to know that I could get a good cup of coffee each morning. Hotel room coffee brewing is usually a bit weak and tasteless. To unpack the drip coffee maker in our RV each day for just one or two cups of coffee just didn't seem worth the effort. My French Press was the perfect answer.

Coffee made in a French Press allows the hot water to come in contact with the raw grounds. By skipping the filter, you're creating a cup of coffee that's richer, more caffeinated, and full of antioxidants. The benefits of coffee are magnified because of the pure method of producing coffee in this way. It has a super concentration of anticancer compounds. It protects your neural health. It is super rich in antioxidants that help promote concentration and recall. Besides these and other health benefits, it just tastes so good. It has an especially strong and robust flavor. It is coffee the way it was intended to be.

I had to read the instructions to make sure I did it exactly right. I even practiced at home a couple of times. Your coffee needs to be ground to a medium coarseness. Measuring the grounds in proportion to the amount of coffee being made is a very important step. You then pour hot water (just off a boil) into the French Press carafe, and you stir the brew with a wooden spoon. Once stirred, you place the plunger unit on top of the pot. With everything in position, you let the coffee brew for four minutes. Then you use slight pressure to gently lower the plunger to the bottom of the pot. Finally, you pour the brewed coffee into your mug for a steaming cup of happiness.

Our lives are similar to these coffee grounds, and God sometimes uses pressure on our lives to produce the results He wants to see in us. First, our lives are coarse and imperfect. We have flaws, hang-ups, and problems. It sometimes feels like we are in hot water, and that we will never be able to survive. God gently takes His plunger of love, and presses the coarse parts down to the bottom. He comforts and nurtures us through it all, giving us just the right amount of time to steep. When His timing is perfect, we are ready to be poured out for His use and glory.

Our Bible study group recently looked at the 2 Corinthians 4:8-9 passage. You see, as believers in what Christ has done for us, we can experience victory in the midst of our trials. Even though we are hard pressed on every side, we are not crushed! Though life perplexes us, we do not have to live in despair. We will never be abandoned or forsaken. We do not need to fear being destroyed, for we have the promise of eternal life. In this particular study, we were encouraged to write our own personal and present circumstances into this scriptural formula, along with our reestablished response in Christ.[4] Some of the ladies came up with the following: I am burdened, but not overwhelmed. I am disappointed, but not dismayed. My all-time favorite was: I am tired, but not dead!

How true these statements can be in our lives when we realize that we must die to ourselves so that Christ's life can be revealed in us. Someone once said, "Life is tough, then we die." But it doesn't end there! We can make it through the tough times, the times of feeling pressed in and pressed down, "because we know that the one who raised the Lord Jesus from the dead will also raise us up

[4] Alsdorf, Debbie. *He is My Freedom*. Colorado: David C. Cook, 2008.

with Jesus and present us with you in his presence" (2 Corinthians 4:14). We can focus on the promise, not the problem, and not lose heart!

I don't know how you would finish this passage for yourself. Maybe you can relate to what Paul wrote. Maybe you resonate with one of the ladies from the Bible study. Perhaps you have your own circumstances that give you opportunity to refocus and establish a new response in Christ. Just remember the French Press. The final result is a steaming cup of happiness. God wants to use your momentary troubles to show His all-surpassing power. Let Him work His renewal in you! Press on, Lord Jesus!

 ## Single-Cup Summary

- No one really wants to be hard pressed on every side.
- We are jars of clay, "cracked pots," if you will.
- Jesus lets His light shine forth as He takes our trials and exchanges death for life, alienation for love, condemnation for mercy and grace.
- God sometimes uses a pressing in and on our lives to produce the results He wants to see in us.
- We must die to ourselves, so Christ's life can be revealed in us.

 ## Grounded in the Word

- 2 Corinthians 4:6-14
- Hebrews 12:10-11
- Romans 6:11

Points to Ponder and Percolate

_____

_____

_____

_____

_____

_____

_____

_____

_____

_____

_____

_____

_____

_____

_____

_____

_____

_____

_____

_____

_____

RUNNING OVER

Give, and it will be given to you. A good measure, pressed down,
shaken together and running over, will be poured into your lap.
Luke 6:38a

 An old Sunday school song courses through my mind as I read this passage in Luke.

Running over, running over,
My cup is full and running over,
Since the Lord saved me,
I'm as happy as can be.
My cup is full and running over.

As a youngster, I'm not sure I fully understood the meaning of this song. Paired with the scripture verse and the joy of my salvation that I have received, I think I am beginning to get it. Our first act of giving is to offer our lives to God. In return we receive His forgiveness, love, grace, peace, and more than a good measure of other blessings. They are poured into us until our lives just overflow with His joy and goodness. The principle of giving transfers to other areas of our lives as well. We observe it in ourselves and in the lives of others.

It's intriguing how life will often come full circle. As a teenager, my husband attended a summer camp at Hume Lake. The speaker for his camp was Jim Tubbs. His message and unemotional yet challenging altar call one evening changed my husband's future. He made a commitment that night to live for Jesus fully, to be all in, to go all out for God. After a couple of moves, we ended up in Bakersfield, on the same Nazarene church district that Jim Tubbs pastored. Thus, as an adult, my husband had a chance to thank Jim for being obedient that night to God's Word and His voice. Jim had given a week of his summer, and the good measure of a life changed was being poured back into his lap decades later.

It's an interesting coincidence that Jim's son attends my brother's church in Southern California. My brother gives to Dave through pastoring and friendship. Dave gives back through being a committed layman in his church. Continuing in this vain, Jim's daughter, Jeri, ended up at our church. We have had some great conversations and fellowship with her, and our church family just prayed over a mission trip Jeri was getting ready to embark on to Africa. I'm sure that she will reap many benefits from her time on this pursuit. It was after a Sunday morning service in April that Jeri came to me and told me her dad had a coffee story. After a couple of emails back and forth, I was thrilled to receive one of Jim's accounts of how God worked in his life over coffee.

One of Jim's calls to give of himself was to pastor the Nazarene church in Hanford, California. When he arrived there, a strategic part of his ministry plans was to visit every home connected to his church. There was a teen girl in the congregation who asked that he not call at her home because her father hated preachers and had no use for religion. She was afraid of the scene it might create

Jim learned that the teen's dad worked a night shift at the local creamery, and each morning, after he got off work, he stopped at a local diner for coffee with his coworkers. Jim began frequenting the diner to read his morning paper and work the crossword puzzle, sitting as close as possible to this group of men as he enjoyed his cup of coffee. Occasionally he would volunteer a comment on what they were discussing. They slowly began to include Jim in their conversation.

As he left the diner one morning, he paid the waitress for the teen's father's coffee. He asked that she not tell him who had paid for it. He continued to sporadically do this. The father finally figured it out, and one morning as Jim was leaving the waitress told him, "Your coffee has been paid for." The next time he was there Jim thanked the dad.

This simple interaction between the two men built a bridge until, more often than not, Jim became a part of the group's morning debrief. After some time, one of the workers asked him about his occupation. Jim replied that he pastored the Nazarene Church. The father of the teen leaned forward, looking around at all the men seated between them at the counter, and smiled at Jim. Through this simple avenue, God was opening this dad's heart. He seemed to sense that there was more to faith and church than he had always thought. Over time, he began attending the Assembly of God Church with his wife and became a staunch Christian. What an amazing return on the initial investment!

Giving of our time, our resources, and our talents, does not ensure that we will become a millionaire. It does mean that we will reap payments on earth that we couldn't imagine. Our life will be full and our blessings will be shaken together and running over. Most of us tend to cling to what we have. We just know that if we give up our time, we will be stretched beyond our abilities. Instead, as our time is given to God, we often find that our day opens up, and we suddenly have notches in our schedule we hadn't been able to carve out previously. We are certain that giving financially will break the bank and leave us destitute. However, when done out of obedience and trust, our budgets balance, and more often than not, we are amazed at God's abundant provisions. We hold tight to our talents, usually out of insecurity or selfish motive. We don't believe we are good enough, or we want to use our abilities according to our own plans. Yet, in the hands of our Father, whatever we use for Him produces far more than we could ever accomplish on our own.

Through creating **common ground** with this teen's father and letting God work in Jim's heart, the price of a couple cups of coffee was being returned in ways that were priceless and eternal. By the way, the teen's father always planted the biggest garden in his community. When he discovered Jim liked okra he came to him to tell him he had a whole row of okra just for him. For years Jim got so much okra from this gentleman that he had to give away baskets full to avoid having it spoil. Even the good measure of okra, shaken together and running over, was poured into his lap. God has a great sense of humor! What a great God we serve!

Single-Cup Summary

- Our first act of giving is to offer our lives to God.
- In return we gain His forgiveness, love, grace, peace, and immeasurably more than we can ask or imagine.
- We can never overestimate God's return on our initial investment.
- In the hands of our Father, whatever we use for Him produces far more than we could ever accomplish on our own.

 ## Grounded in the Word

- Luke 6:38
- Ephesians 3:20-21
- 2 Corinthians 9:6-11
- Malachi 3:10

Points to Ponder and Percolate

_____

_____

_____

_____

_____

_____

_____

_____

_____

_____

_____

_____

_____

_____

_____

_____

_____

_____

_____

_____

_____

PREPARATION

*But in your hearts set apart Christ as Lord. Always be prepared
to give an answer to everyone who asks you to give a reason for the
hope you have. But do this with gentleness and respect. 1 Peter 3:15*

The preparations had been made. The idyllic setting
in the Blue Ridge Mountains had been procured months
in advance. The grass had been mowed. The plans had
been laid. In spite of the pouring rain earlier in the week, the long
anticipated day dawned with blue skies and spotty clouds. The
friends and family were seated, and the wedding began. It was as
close to perfect as a bride and groom could dream!

We were privileged to make it to this wedding, across the nation
from our California home. The groom, Tyler, a third cousin, had
extended the invitation. Our connection with Tyler, though distant
in residence and relationship, was unique. As a young boy, my
husband had looked up to his cousin, about ten years his senior. His
cousin married and had three boys who eventually modeled for our
three sons how to take sports and faith seriously. Tyler was the
third generation in this family tree, and we all continued to share
holidays and special events together.

As the ceremony began, it was obvious that this couple loved
God. It permeated the vows and the prayers. It was evident in the
tears of joy and the emotion from them both. During the reception,
the best man gave a moving toast. He spoke about the character of

both the bride and groom. He described how they lived intentionally and spontaneously. He gave examples of their inclusive spirits and their vulnerability. All of these things were part of their mission-minded hearts. He told a special story about how Tyler and Sydney had created **common ground** with a Muslim waitress.

The couple later relayed their encounter in greater detail, giving deeper perspective and insight into their hearts. In January of 2018, they went to a Greek restaurant not too far from their university to enjoy a gyro for lunch. They were engaged at the time, and it would have been easy to be totally caught up with each other. Instead, they noticed their server. She was an excellent attendant, but they were intrigued by her strong accent. When they asked where she was from, she told them she had moved here from Egypt.

About halfway through their meal, they noticed that she was on her knees behind the counter, praying, occasionally lifting her hands in the air. This went on for about five minutes. Nobody else was in this small restaurant. Tyler and Sydney, almost simultaneously, felt compelled to pray that the Lord would speak through them to tell her about Jesus.

When she stood up and asked about their food, they began to engage in a conversation. Tyler told her he was studying to be a Christian Pastor. He then asked what religion she practiced. She explained that she was Muslim and that she reads the Quran, Torah, Injil, and the Bible. She told them she prayed to God every day that He would show her children the truth. After listening to her for a while, Tyler and Sydney were able to share what they believe. Sydney told her they only read the Bible. They asked what she believed about Jesus. Throughout the questions and answers they were praying silently that this young woman would know Jesus as her King as a result of this conversation.

For the sake of privacy, we will call the waitress Nailah. Nailah said she believed that Jesus was a prophet; she believed in His second coming, but she didn't believe that Jesus is God. She believed that there is only one God. Since she didn't accept the trinity, she didn't believe that Jesus could have been present at the creation.

Nailah went on to say that she couldn't believe God was tortured. This opened up the opportunity for Tyler to share that Christ suffered because of God's great love for her. He went on to explain that the Bible says the sins of man are forgiven through shedding of blood. That's why Jesus came down to earth. He lived as man, while still 100% God, and shed His own blood for the sins of everyone in the world. Tyler referenced John 14:6 where Jesus says that He is the One Way. He explained the way the Bible teaches to be saved is through having faith in Jesus.

Sydney was very burdened for Nailah. She couldn't shake the intense urgency she felt to follow up their conversation with action. The next day, she bought a Bible, highlighted some verses in it, and drove back to the restaurant to give it to Nailah. Nailah was very surprised to see Sydney as she walked in during her busy lunch hour. She asked if she could touch and hold the Bible. She even washed her hands and used a napkin to hold it. She clearly understood that this was a Holy book and should not be handled recklessly. At first she wouldn't accept such a huge gift from a stranger, but Sydney explained that they had specifically bought the book for her and had even written her name in the front cover.

Sydney asked permission to explain the perspective of the book to her, clarifying that it would not make sense to her if she read it from a Muslim perspective. Nailah was very excited and eager to gain understanding of Christian beliefs and this new book that she had received. Sydney began going through the key verses that she had highlighted for her from Genesis to Revelation and explained key characteristics of God and his actions throughout history. After much conversation about how we as people fit into this grand narrative, Sydney prayed for Nailah and left her with the suggestion to begin reading the book of John.

Tyler and Sydney have been back numerous times to stop and see Nailah. They pray with her, making sure to start the prayer by saying "Dear Jesus." They continue to pray that Nailah will be their sister in Christ as she continues to search for answers in her life.

Until now, the older cousins had influenced the younger cousins in our family. Here was an obvious reversal in roles. This young couple was a shining example of living out their faith in their world. Their passion and willingness to engage in spiritual conversations was inspiring. We can all learn from them and their boldness to share their faith with those who are seeking to find The Way. Here are a few take-aways:

- "Do not be despised because of your youth" (1 Timothy 4:12). It doesn't matter how old or young you are, how experienced or inexperienced you are. God can use you to minister to the lost!
- It's so much easier to have a conversation about what people believe than you think. Simple questions go a long way. "The Holy Spirit will teach you at that time what you should say" (Luke 12:12).

- It's essential to actually care about and listen to what someone else believes to be true if you want them to listen when you share.
- You can't shy away from the truth of Scripture. Someone may be close to the Truth, but miss THE aspect of the Gospel, Jesus. Communicate that you just don't believe in good morals as the way to salvation.
- The Gospel is offensive to those who do not believe in it. It is important to know what you believe and why you believe it! Be prepared with your answer (see I Timothy 4:12)!

In *Organic Outreach for Ordinary People*, Kevin Harney encourages us to have as many tools in our outreach toolbox as we possibly can. He says, "We should be able to share the message of Jesus in many different ways."[5] This takes preparation and practice. It's not about a memorized speech, but having a variety of ways to share the message of the gospel. We need to know what we believe, and be ready to talk and pray with people about what God has done and is doing. Our prayer should constantly be for boldness, humility, and readiness to tell others about the hope He has unleashed in our lives.

---

[5] Harney, Kevin G. *Organic Outreach for Ordinary People, Sharing Good News Naturally.* Grand Rapids, Michigan: Zondervan, 2009. 224-225

Single-Cup Summary

- When we take the time to listen to what others believe, they will be more receptive to listen to us about our faith.
- Jesus is the one Way to be saved.
- We can learn from the examples and boldness of those younger than us.
- It's important to be prepared to share the hope that lies within us, but when the time comes, the Holy Spirit will teach us what to say.

 ## Grounded in the Word

- 1 Peter 3:13–16
- John 14:6
- 1 Timothy 4:12
- Luke 12:12

Points to Ponder and Percolate

BABU COFFEE

"For I know the plans I have for you," declares the Lord, "plans to prosper you and not to harm you, plans to give you a hope and a future." Jeremiah 29:11

Randy Martin's connection with coffee began early. His mom recognized that caffeine tended to have an opposite effect on her young, active little boy, so she began to regularly invite him to have a cup of coffee with her in the morning. The coffee would be laced with sugar and cream so that it seemed like a treat to him. This opportunity to create **common ground** with his mom was vital.

Randy forgot about coffee for a few years. He even thought it was a poor excuse for a beverage. Then one morning in Seattle, after a long night, he became acquainted with a coffee cart as he was trying to get ready for a family function. The barista fixed him an espresso, and his world changed! Eventually Randy bought his own coffee cart in Bakersfield and called it Crossroads Coffee. He took it to a variety of venues to share his new-found passion.

The coffee cart eventually became a ministry opportunity as he worked with Canyon Hills Assembly of God Church. He would show up at youth events, Jesus Shack, or wherever God directed him. God was stirring up a perfect storm in Randy's life. At around this same time, Randy and his wife answered a call during a church service to work with foster youth in a camp setting. By 1999,

Randy's focus shifted to working with foster children. They donated the coffee cart to Olive Knolls Nazarene Church.

Around 2006, the twelve and thirteen-year-old foster kids they had worked with were now eighteen to twenty-year-old young adults. They were finding themselves suddenly thrust into the real world, with nowhere to go and very little direction. As they contacted Randy, he and his wife began to develop mentoring programs for these emancipated youth. They helped secure housing, but finding jobs was another obstacle. Most of the youth were in a cycle of not having enough experience or education to get a job, and without a job they didn't have the means to get the experience and education they needed. They had no resumes, little skill sets, and minimal understanding of what it meant to be a good employee.

Randy and his ministry team decided that they would become the place that would hire youth and give them "fourteen chances until they got it right." As they looked around Bakersfield, they tried to determine a business avenue that was not already being used in the area. They realized that no one was roasting coffee. This was a specialty market that they could latch on to for launching this new venture. God placed the right people in their path to train and serve. Covenant Coffee was born. Eventually they procured a brick-and-mortar building that they could use to house their coffee roaster equipment, the coffee shop itself, and meeting rooms and offices.

Through experience, and a God-given vision, they realized that coffee was a vehicle in which they could connect with people. The longer they could hang out with people, the more discipleship they could do. Through the foster care's case management system, their contact with youth had been limited in time and scope. Now they could work with them all day long. It became more than just a job. It was a chance to do some intensive discipleship and work with them through problems they faced. It was a safe place for them to have meetings and conversations every single day. In addition they were providing life skills, vocational training, and job experience.

Randy Martin, CEO of Covenant Community Services, still connects through coffee. Many people do not realize that their coffee shop is not just about great coffee. It is a ministry that works with one hundred to one hundred fifty youth daily. Randy knows that most people will get up in the morning and reach for their cup of coffee. Most would not have in the forefront of their mind that they will go out and touch a foster youth that day. Paying a visit to Covenant Coffee allows you to be a part of the ministry motto, "Hope lives here." Enjoying a cup of their fresh roasted coffee is truly "Hope in a cup." Their unique location allows them to minister to a community that needs Jesus. It is a redeeming place. Throughout our conversation, Randy described coffee as a vehicle, an open door, and a sideshow to God showing up in so many ways!

I asked Randy to share a breakthrough story. After a little thought, he landed on Kenny. Kenny had brought us through the store to Randy's office that morning, so I knew who he was talking about. Kenny started in their program with a bang at age eighteen. He was doing great until about twenty-one, when he began to question things and get in a slump spiritually, physically, and emotionally. Eventually he came back, straightened out, and Kenny became their assistant roaster. He fell off the map again, got in some trouble with the wrong crowd, was involved in some gang activity, and was homeless for a while. They brought him back yet again, and he stuck around. He now manages the program he lived in and bounced out of twice. He's going back to school, bought his first car, doing a great job at Covenant, and is mentoring and training other youth there.

The lovingkindness of God, mixed with the perseverance of His love, is a key to the ministry of Covenant Coffee. Kenny's life changed when he understood that God would not stop the chase. It took a people group like the Covenant family to exhibit Christ's love and grace and mercy. The enemy wanted to trap Kenny in his master plan to steal, kill, and destroy, (see John 10:10). He wants to ruin generations who live in a cycle of child abuse and neglect and being removed from the family unit. The "Kennys" of this world do not want that life, but they don't know any other way. The shame the guilt, and the stigma has followed these kids who are now exited from the system. The enemy says, "I know the plans I have for you...plans to live a hopeless life!"

Randy said you have to meet them back at the table and say the same thing again and again and again. You must love deeply, until it hurts. There is not an off day with God where He says He doesn't love you. Neither can we have a day where we give up or stop loving. Covenant's ministry is based on three action based movement statements: 1) Give hope always. 2) Support with love and accountability. 3) Provide opportunity for growth. As the staff stay on their knees and remain true to their mission and calling, they watch God show up. They get to see the lightbulb come on as these young adults start to realize God's answer to their lives: "'For I know the plans I have for you,' declares the Lord, 'plans to prosper you and not to harm you, plans to give you a hope and a future'" (Jeremiah 29:11).

The fond remembrance of his morning coffee with his mom has spurred Randy to start a similar tradition with his grandkids. He calls it "Babu coffee." Babu, Randy's grandpa name, is German for a loved one, one who loves unconditionally. Each grandchild has their own espresso mug with their name on it. The **common ground** he is establishing with his beloved as they drink coffee together, laced with plenty of sugar and cream, is already reaching far into their future and deep down into their hearts.

 ## Single-Cup Summary

- We need to give others "fourteen chances" until they get it right.
- The enemy wants to steal, kill, and destroy, creating a hopeless cycle in our lives.
- We can't have a day where we stop loving.
- Jesus came that we may have life, a hope, and a future.

 ## Grounded in the Word

- Jeremiah 29:11
- Matthew 18:21-22
- John 10:10
- 1 Corinthians 13

Points to Ponder and Percolate

_____

_____

_____

_____

_____

_____

_____

_____

_____

_____

_____

_____

_____

_____

_____

_____

_____

_____

_____

_____

_____

_____

SAVED BY GRACE

For it is by grace you have been saved, through faith—and this not from yourselves, it is the gift of God—not by works, so that no one can boast. Ephesians 2:8-9

Richard Newton doesn't drink coffee, but he fixes his wife, Tiffany's, coffee each morning. He experimented with various brands and measurements until she agreed that it was the way she liked it. Each morning he gets up early and prepares her perfect cup. This is how Richard lives his life. He is selfless and full of grace.

Richard is the facilities manager at Olive Knolls Nazarene Church. He oversees the comings and goings of groups and events, making sure the campus is safe and ready. Besides his dedication to his job, he is a devoted member of the church and its ministries. Over the years he has allowed God to direct him into leading Bible studies and small groups. God seems to keep nudging him into relationships with teens and young adults.

For about 5 years Richard lead his college-aged daughter and her friends through the Word. Their home was a place of refuge. These young adults could ask questions in a non-judgmental environment. They had a safe place to hang out for New Year's Eve or Friday nights to try to keep away from the partying scene. Some resided for a period of time with Richard and his wife, and many of the twenty-five or so kids would call him "dad."

In the past several years, Richard's ministry has landed at "The Landing." This is the teen portion of Celebrate Recovery (CR), a place where people learn to confront their hurts, habits and hang-ups and place them into God's hands. Richard didn't always lead this group. He was facilitating adult groups until God pointed him in a different direction.

At a CR training in Southern California, Richard had looked at the breakout sessions and circled several that he hoped to attend. When the time came for Breakout #1, he went to the first choice on his list. It was full. Similarly, his second and third choices had reached their capacity, and he was turned away. Sitting on a bench in the hallway, Richard was contemplating what to do when God prompted him to try the door directly across from where he was seated. He had no idea what was behind the door, but he opened it. Immediately he was welcomed and received into a training on "The Landing."

Richard relates that his heart so resonated with the things that were being taught and shared about reaching the young people, that he rearranged the rest of his schedule to go to more classes regarding this aspect of the CR program. Upon returning to Olive Knolls, he decided to just go and sit in on The Landing session, which already had two adult leaders. When the leaders asked him why he was there, he explained his interest, but assured them he knew they had it covered. The two men looked at each other, then back at Richard. This was one of the guys' last nights, and they had been praying that God would bring the right person to fill the void. The transition was made, and God confirmed the open doors that He had been guiding Richard through.

It was in this setting that Richard met Donovan. At seventeen Donovan had already faced tough circumstances. His parents were both drug abusers, and his dad had been in and out of prison. He was tired of trying to make things work, so he came with one of his friends to the Friday night Celebrate Recovery session. For Donovan, it was just a way to get away from his environment. He didn't really have any intention of opening up or working on himself. He was rough around the edges and in a lot of personal pain, but he was content at the moment to keep it covered and pushed down deep inside.

Over the next few weeks, Donovan began to gain trust in the group. He realized that each person had issues they were dealing with, and his sarcastic responses began to be more genuine. His answers became more wrought with emotion, and the pain began to come out. Richard began to take Donovan and his friend home after the sessions, so that they would have more time to build their relationship. Richard felt a strong connection and wanted to nurture it. He realized that Donovan had not had much of a father figure, and perhaps God could use him to stand in the gap for Donovan.

Eventually, Richard offered Donovan a chance to work part time on the weekends with church service set-up and tear-down. This gave Donovan some purpose, plus it allowed for their relationship to further develop. Richard would talk to Donovan like a son, challenging him and loving him unconditionally. One Sunday, as they were waiting for the second morning service to end so they could get to work on taking down the chairs, Donovan had a breakthrough.

Pastor Darren was preaching about how God shows us an open door to His love and goodness. We stand on the threshold or look in from afar, but we tend to stay on the side with which we are the most familiar. We don't want to leave our comfort zone to be all in with Christ. Even though we may be convinced that He has our best in mind, the uncertainties of what we might have to give up or change keeps us from entering the door. Before Richard knew what had happened, Donovan was making a bee-line for the altar. He made a decision to follow Christ's plan for his life, and the two men prayed for Donovan to allow the door to close behind him and not look back.

When Donovan was baptized, we all rejoiced over his testimony. As he made his profession of faith public, the congregation cheered and promised to pray for him! Due to some frightening and disheartening situations on the home front, Donovan was invited to stay in Richard and Tiffany's home. He began working full time at the church facility. He reached out to his mom to try and rebuild their relationship, as she is working to stay clean.

As with anyone, Donovan's new walk with Jesus is filled with ups and downs. Richard sometimes has to have difficult conversations with him, to encourage him to stay on the right path. In his enthusiasm for his new found faith, Donovan was frustrated that his friends weren't falling in line. One of the things Richard shared with Donovan was that **we** don't save anyone. We can tell people about Jesus and what He has done in our lives, but it is God and His grace that saves. Donovan was encouraged to let his consistent actions and changed life lead others to God. Richard communicated that God has taught him that we extend grace to others because of the measure of grace He has shown to us.

We live in a world that is hurting and in pain. Through the gift of God's grace, we can draw others to Him. There is nothing any of us can do to earn our way into God's favor. It is because of our own depravity that we are drawn to accept God's grace at some point in our lives. When we recognize how much He did for us, we realize that there is no room for us to be judgmental. We can only extend as much grace to others as was extended to us, and that's eternally greater than anything we can ever imagine.

 ## Single-Cup Summary

- The interruptions in our plans are often God's way of closing a door and opening another.
- We must decide to leave our comfort zone and walk through the door Christ has opened for us.
- We extend grace to others because of the measure of grace God has shown to us.

 ## Grounded in the Word

- Ephesians 2:8-9
- Proverbs 16:9
- Revelation 3:7-8
- Luke 6:36

Points to Ponder and Percolate

A COFFEE VOW

I will fulfill my vows to the Lord in the presence of all his people. Psalm 116:14

In Psalm 116, King David is referring to his vow to call on the name of the Lord and to give Him thanks and praise. In an earlier Psalm, David makes this commitment: "I will give thanks to the Lord because of his righteousness and will sing praise to the name of the Lord Most High" (Psalm 7:17). Throughout the one-hundred-fifty chapters found in the Psalms, David kept his vow! He praised God when things were going well, and he gave thanks when he was overwhelmed with problems.

Oaths and vows in Biblical time were taken very seriously. A person's word was his bond, and he was expected to do everything he said (see Numbers 30:2). In the New Testament Jesus admonished us to let our "Yes" be "Yes," and our "No" be "No" (See Matthew 5:37).

Too often we find ourselves making a promise, an oath, a vow, but then find that we can no longer keep it. Many a marriage vow is initially made with heartfelt commitment, but that promise is broken when the couple "falls out of love." We promise ourselves, and even sometimes God, that we will give up a bad habit, or never turn away from Him. Then we are faced with a temptation, and our will slips and fails. Fortunately we serve a God who redeems us.

When we repent and count on Him to get us through our temptations and failures, He is faithful to forgive and to help.

My brother, the youngest of three siblings, made a vow to serve God. He followed a call to become a pastor, and has allowed God to use him for several decades in this capacity. It has been fun to see my little brother, Jimbo, as we called him, grow in his love and devotion to his family, his church, and primarily to God. He recently shared with me about another vow he made, a vow to stop drinking coffee. It is best told in his words:

It has almost been ten years since I gave up drinking coffee, a habit I was quite fond of for the previous thirty years. So, what happened?

A young man, the son of a single woman by divorce, that had grown up in the church I'm the pastor of had become addicted to drugs. His journey to the dark side of the drug culture started at least in High School and became progressively complicated with an addiction that caused him to steal from his own mother and others and to act out, sometimes violently, when he was under the influence.

Our church had come alongside this single mom, a nurse by profession, back in the days that the new show, "Extreme Home Makeover," was a hit. Her home was in need of repairs that our church body could assist with, including repairing several holes in the walls that her son had made in fits of rage.

Circumstances continued to get worse for the young man as he deepened in his addiction without seeking help. He had multiple vehicle accidents that further destroyed his ability to function in a productive way in society. He also was in and out of our local mental health hospital for attempts at suicide. Ultimately, he ended up in trouble with the law and spent some time in jail. In each of these progressively worse episodes I had the privilege of trying to respond to the young man and his mom in a pastoral way.

The court system required him to enroll in a rehab program, and after several stints with that and then falling back into the addiction, he enrolled with a rehab organization run by a local Calvary Chapel.

I went to visit him at this facility that had a very structured program. It was clear that he was serious about trying to get healthy this time. Somewhere in our conversation I was attempting to sympathize with what it must be like to be addicted to something so powerful.

It hit me at that moment of how I was actually addicted to that wonderful morning aroma of freshly brewed coffee. I enjoyed my cups of coffee throughout the day. I would brew four measuring cups according to the markings on the carafe, and drink that to wake up. I would then go to the office and have another couple of mugs worth during the day. Then I would typically brew four more measuring cups for my evening at home.

I realized how addicted I was on a weekend winter camp with our church youth group. We had rented a Seventh Day Adventist campground and I did not realize they did not partake in caffeine. There was some kind of instant coffee they had available, but it was decaffeinated. It took no time at all before I was in withdrawal. The headaches were truly painful. I didn't sleep well all weekend. I was grumpy and mean on a retreat that was supposed to be focusing on spiritual growth. I grew the wrong way. Getting out of that camp after three days was glorious.

During my visit at the Calvary Chapel rehab facility, as we talked about addiction, I made a vow to this young man that I would stop drinking coffee while he was going through the rehab so I could try to share his experience at least in a mild way.

At first the days were long. My headaches returned like those I had at that weekend retreat. My disposition was not very becoming of a follower of Christ who was doing this action for spiritual reasons. The first week was awful. This must be what Hell is like. Actually, probably not, but I'm a preacher and we tend to embellish our stories at times.

The weeks soon became months. During this time, I became quite fond of heating water and putting it in my coffee mugs. I soon was drinking hot water as much as I had been drinking coffee. I enjoyed the warmth of the mug in my hands, especially on colder days and early in the morning.

Four months passed and the young man had been sober the entire time and was feeling good about his progress. As part of the program the residents at the Calvary Chapel rehab facility would attend the local Calvary Chapel for Sunday services. He was making spiritual progress, memorizing required scripture passages, and staying involved in daily Bible Studies.

It was at this time that the residents of the rehab facility were given the opportunity to be baptized at a huge baptismal service the church was having. It was going to be in the waters of the Pacific Ocean at a beach in Southern California.

The young man from our church decided to be baptized and told his mom. His mom told several of us in our Home Bible Study Group, and on the day of his baptism, about fifteen of us went to the party.

Just before it was his turn to go into the water, I was talking with this young man about my journey of no coffee for the past four months. I suggested, "Now that you are being baptized I guess I will be able to return to my daily coffee routine." He just looked at me quietly for what seemed like a few minutes and then said, "You can't do that because I can't go back to Heroin."

It hit me hard. He had a valid point. I had no concept when I made my original vow that I was making a lifelong commitment. My conviction was relentless, and here I am nearly 10 years later completely addicted to multiple cups of hot water every day. I went ahead and gave up soda, another former pleasure, and I seldom drink anything except water.

My wife just thinks I'm weird and typically gets embarrassed when we are at a restaurant and I ask for a cup of hot water and a glass of cold water. Many of my friends just think I'm boring. But for me, it has been an intriguing adventure as I try to understand what it is like to deal with an addiction for the rest of my life. I have a deep respect for those who are living sober, whose addictions have much deeper consequences. It has been a spiritual journey that has helped me with other disciplines that I have come to value deeply as well.

The other lesson in all this is... be careful what you commit to and make vows to do. Life is already not so easy. I really have no regrets. I do confess that I will occasionally order a Starbucks Tall Coffee Frappuccino with whip when I am on a long driving trip, but I also order a cup of hot water to cleanse immediately after that delightful falling off the wagon. Is that called a chaser?

I still enjoy the smell of freshly brewed coffee, but my dentist is pretty impressed with the lack of staining on my teeth. Believe me, I'm not doing this for the dentist. My life desire is to please God and He is the One who created coffee plants... so you don't need to feel like you should take this as seriously as I do. I roasted myself on this one.

I can think of no greater vow, other than living for Jesus, than to come along side someone who needs understanding and support. I'm sure this looks, feels, and sounds differently for as many situations as there are people and relationships. Maybe your vow is to pray for someone daily. Maybe your promise is to help a single mom in need. Say "yes" to Jesus and His call on your life, and remember to always thank and praise Him in all circumstances. But do not take your commitment lightly. You will not have any regrets as you work to please the God who created you!

 ## Single-Cup Summary

- We should call on the name of the Lord and give Him thanks and praise in all circumstances.
- When we make a vow before God, we should treat it seriously and allow God to help us persevere in our commitment.
- Look for those God may entrust to you who may need understanding and support.
- We will have no regrets as we work to please the God who created us and press on toward the goal for which He has called us.

 ## Grounded in the Word

- Psalm 116:12-14
- Psalm 7:17
- 1 Thessalonians 5:16-18
- Matthew 5:37
- Philippians 3:12-14

Points to Ponder and Percolate

NOT THE END

The Word became flesh and made his dwelling among us.
John 1:14a

Since I started this *Common Ground* project, I have become more intricately aware of coffee shop names, coffee sayings, and the coffee culture in general. A few coffee houses have already been mentioned in previous chapters, but a few of the places I have been able to visit in our recent travels are:

- Common Grounds
- ReFresh
- Cornerstone
- Rushmore Roasters
- Maverick
- Calamity Jane (more on that later)
- Hume 'n' Bean

I have seen sayings on t-shirts, wooden signs, and coffee cups such as:
- "May your coffee be stronger than your toddler." (Another t-shirt replaced teenager for toddler—whatever fits, wear it)
- "It's 7 AM somewhere."
- "Today's good mood is sponsored by coffee."
- "I may not cry over spilled milk, but I'll lose my mind over spilled coffee!"
- "Coffee is like a hug in a mug"

- DEPRESSO—the feeling you get when you're out of coffee

The coffee obsession doesn't end with clever store designations and cute mottos. A recent article in a mail circular explained how you can get cooking with coffee. They explained how to use coffee in baked goods, meat rubs, marinades, and soups. They offered a few recipes and encouraged the reader to try it in just about any dish. The article also explained that August is National Coffee Month, and September 29 is National Coffee Day. Though not an official act of Congress, someone arbitrarily assigned these dates to celebrate the already popular beverage. I'm sure coffee establishments will take advantage of these dates to promote their products.

It wasn't National Coffee Month, but in June, in Custer, South Dakota, I spoke with the owner of the Calamity Jane. We talked for quite a while about how he started serving coffee at his mercantile in this quaint historic town. He admitted to having become obsessed with coffee: its flavors, its roasting methods, its draw to people. For him every month was coffee month. We ended up purchasing a locally roasted coffee from him. The alleged story behind the name of the business is that Calamity Jane had worked as a dishwasher in that exact location, when the building was a restaurant and saloon housed in a gold rush era tent. We couldn't confirm the story, but it was a fun conversation!

Another place in South Dakota that had been recommended to us by several people was Wall Drug, in Wall, South Dakota. This town, population 872 (2016 census) receives more than two million visitors each year. They offer coffee for five cents, and you pay for it by placing a coin in a wooden box when you pour your cup. It's completely on the honor system. But the real reason they began attracting so many visitors in the 1930's is because they advertised and offered free ice water to travelers.

The story goes that Dorothy and Ted Hustead had moved to Wall to try to run a drug store and pharmaceutical business. They decided to give it five years to succeed. Toward the end of the fifth year, they were discouraged and about to give up. That's when Dorothy had the idea of putting up signs along the highway offering free ice water to hot, weary travelers. Within days of posting the signs, people began to pour in, and visitors have not stopped coming since. They still offer free ice water, and their price for coffee has not gone up. This simple concept grew their store to a complex that occupies a city block. The town has also reaped many benefits from the added tourists.

The key behind most successful coffee businesses is the customer service they provide to enhance your coffee experience. The Starbuck's philosophy and customer connection is intriguing. Their mission statement is this:

> *To inspire and nurture the human spirit – one person, one cup and one neighborhood at a time.*

They strive to live these values:

- **Creating a culture of warmth and belonging, where everyone is welcome.**
- **Acting with courage, challenging the status quo and finding new ways to grow our company and each other.**
- **Being present, connecting with transparency, dignity and respect.**
- **Delivering our very best in all we do, holding ourselves accountable for results.**

As they train their employees they give them a *Green Apron Book*—a small booklet meant to fit in the pocket of a barista's apron. It outlines five ways of being: Be genuine; Be considerate; Be welcoming; Be knowledgeable; Be involved. Their outline for customer service is: Connect, Discover and Respond.

If we lived our Christian walk with some of these core values and ideas, we might just revolutionize our world! Our "Green Apron Book" is God's Word, and it trains us according to His values and mission. How God could use us to connect with others, whether over coffee or over a meal, if we were genuinely considerate and welcoming, striving to get to know others and love them unconditionally, sharing life-giving truth with them!

The reason creating **common ground** with others is so effective is because it was modeled for us through Christ's walk on this earth. He knew that creating relationships around conversations and time together was key to helping others find out who the Father really was and is. In order to draw people to Himself, Jesus had to open Himself up to others and be willing to listen and care about them.

When Jesus became flesh and dwelt among us, his first miracle was at a wedding celebration, not in the temple. He developed intimacy and respect with his disciples over a fish barbeque on the beach. He ate with tax collectors in their homes, where they were most comfortable. He spoke to the woman at the well, the natural gathering place of the time, about the living water that she so desperately needed. He fed multitudes on a hillside and met regularly over meals in the home of Martha, Mary and Lazarus.

He showed us how to love and serve others so that their hearts would be open to Him.

Coffee is just an avenue. There are so many ways you can reach out to your friends, neighbors, co-workers, and acquaintances. I hope some of these thoughts, these real-life accounts, these truths from Scripture, will spur you on to begin or strengthen your life with Christ. I certainly desire that you will be inspired to reach out to some of your circle of influence and be more intentional about creating **common ground**.

"In the beginning God created the Heavens and the earth...In the beginning was the Word...and the Word became flesh and dwelt among us" (Genesis 1:1, John 1:1a, John 1:4a). It has been God's plan since the fall of mankind in the Garden of Eden to reestablish communion between us and Him. Jesus made the ultimate sacrifice, His life, to be the atonement for our sins. He wants to use those who have accepted His gift of salvation to spread this Good News. You can begin by opening yourself up to others and being willing to listen and care about them. Whether it's over a cup of coffee or tea, at a baseball game, or at a neighborhood barbeque, you can follow Jesus's example by creating **common ground**. Write your own story! This is not The End!

Single-Cup Summary

- Creating **common ground** originated with God and was modeled for us by Jesus during His time on Earth.
- It has been God's plan since the beginning to restore fellowship between us and Him.
- Like Jesus, reach out to your circle of influence and create **common ground.**
- Write your own story!

 ## Grounded in the Word

- John 1:14
- John 2:1-11
- John 4:1-26
- Mark 2:15
- Matthew 14:13-21
- Luke 10:38-42
- Psalm 23:3

Points to Ponder and Percolate